This is a very good book
interest in contemporary
of the current state of Indigenous politics. What is more, it is
highly readable and a superb synthesis of many diverse
sources.

*Professor Henry Reynolds, ARC Professorial
Fellow, School of History & Classics, University of Tasmania*

Action is urgently needed in Australia to right old wrongs, many of which have not been fully corrected. Larissa Behrendt repeats an important lesson in a new context: Think globally; act locally. Some may disagree with her solutions. None can doubt the importance of her questions.

Hon Justice Michael Kirby AC CMG

Australia aspires to be a confident, multicultural nation. But we face the challenge of ensuring the compatibility of our legal system and Aboriginal culture. Larissa Behrendt's insights and erudition combine in this work of interest and reference.

Gerard Brennan, Chancellor UTS

This is indispensable reading for anyone who hungers to hear of a pathway beyond the empty conservative rhetoric of practical reconciliation. If you desire genuine reconciliation, this book provides guidelines.

Julia Gillard MP, Shadow Minister for Reconciliation & Indigenous Affairs

Far too much energy and resources have been expended in trying to restrict and limit the application of any Indigenous rights that are recognised in Australia. We should instead be looking at how those rights will enable strong economic foundations for Indigenous people today. *Achieving Social Justice* is a valuable contribution to this discussion.

Senator Aden Ridgeway, Australian Democrats Spokesperson on Indigenous Affairs

Achieving Social Justice is a magnificent synthesis of Indigenous history and insights as they relate to Indigenous people, human rights and law. Based in profound scholarship yet highly readable and accessible, it deserves the widest possible readership.

Dr William Jonas AM, Aboriginal and Torres Strait Islander Social Justice Commissioner, Human Rights and Equal Opportunity Commission

In this remarkably lucid and readable book, Larissa Behrendt urges an approach to Indigenous claims and demands which is far-sighted and principled. Behrendt focuses on what Indigenous people actually say they want, and especially what they mean by 'sovereignty' and 'self-determination'. *Achieving Social Justice* suggests new ways forward in Indigenous affairs. With proposals that are both ambitious in the long term and yet specific and realistic in the shorter term, this book will help set the agenda for future debate.

Professor Ann Curthoys, Manning Clark Professor of History, Australian National University, and author of Freedom Ride: A Freedomrider Remembers

This book, by an exceptional academic, is important because it is suffused by her Aboriginal perspective. What is important about [it] is that it is a clear and unambiguous statement of what is wrong with the status quo from an Aboriginal perspective. It helps to define the unfinished business of reconciliation.

Fred Chaney, Co-Chairperson of Reconciliation Australia

A powerful and personal narrative of why reconciliation is vital to Australia's future. Larissa Behrendt is one of Australia's leading young thinkers on Indigenous law and policy. Her book is a provocative and timely contribution.

Professor George Williams, Anthony Mason Professor and Director, Gilbert & Tobin Centre of Public Law, University of New South Wales

Achieving social justice

Dr Larissa Behrendt is Professor of Law at the University of Technology, Sydney, where she is also Director of the Jumbunna Indigenous House of Learning. She was the first Australian Aboriginal to obtain a doctorate from Harvard Law School; the winner of the Inaugural Neville Bonner National Teaching Award in 2002; and was described in March 2002 in *The Australian* as one of the leading lights of the next generation of Australia's Indigenous leaders.

Her first book, *Aboriginal Dispute Resolution*, was published by the Federation Press in 1995 when she was 25 years old. *Achieving Social Justice*, which developed out of her work at Harvard, is her second. Her third will be a novel, *Home*, the winner of the 2002 David Unaipon Award for an unpublished manuscript, to be published by the University of Queensland Press. She is currently working on a manuscript emerging out of the Eliza Fraser story and its treatment in Australian literature.

Achieving social justice

Indigenous rights and Australia's future

Larissa Behrendt

THE FEDERATION PRESS
2003

Published in Sydney by:
 The Federation Press
 PO Box 45, Annandale, NSW, 2038
 71 John St, Leichhardt, NSW, 2040
 Ph (02) 9552 2200 Fax (02) 9552 1681
 E-mail: info@federationpress.com.au
 Website: http://www.federationpress.com.au

National Library of Australia
Cataloguing-in-Publication entry

 Behrendt, Larissa.
 Achieving Social Justice: indigenous rights
 and Australia's future

 Bibliography.
 Includes index.
 ISBN 1 86287 450 6

 1. Aborigines, Australian – Civil rights. 2. Torres Strait Islanders – Civil rights. 3. Aborigines, Australian – Government policy. 4. Torres Strait Islanders – Government policy. 5. Aborigines, Australian – Legal status laws etc. 5. Torres Strait Islanders – Legal status, laws etc.
 I. Title.

323.119915

© The Federation Press

This publication is copyright. Other than for the purposes of and subject to the conditions prescribed under the Copyright Act, no part of it may in any form or by any means (electronic, mechanical, microcopying, photocopying, recording or otherwise) be reproduced, stored in a retrieval system or transmitted without prior written permission. Enquiries should be addressed to the publishers.

Typeset by The Federation Press, Leichhardt, NSW.
 Printed by Southwood Press Pty Ltd, Marrickville, NSW.

For Roberto Mangabeira Unger

and

Kris Faller

It is true that we cannot be visionaries until we become realists. It is also true that to become realists we must make ourselves into visionaries.

Roberto Mangabeira Unger

Contents

	Acknowledgments	xi
1	**Why question the rules?**	1
	Australians and the first Australians	7
	Practical reconciliation or the rights agenda?	9
	A belief in substantive equality	13
	More than a 'noisy minority'	14
	The concept of democracy	16
	New approaches to Indigenous rights protection	18
2	**The myth of law's neutrality: Why formal equality doesn't work**	21
	Different conceptions of justice	21
	Different conceptions of property	31
	Different conceptions of equality	54
3	**Nationalism and identity: Why 'Western' institutions don't work for everyone**	56
	The Australian self-image	57
	Challenging the Australian self-image	67
	Why recognition matters	76

4	**Indigenous aspirations: The starting point for rights protection**	**86**
	What 'Indigenous sovereignty' and 'Indigenous self-determination' might mean	87
	Deciphering the content of Indigenous sovereignty and self-determination	103
	The parameters of Indigenous claims	115
5	**New strategies, improved rights protection**	**118**
	A program for institutional change	120
	Indigenous rights and aspirations	123
	Some underlying principles	125
6	**Towards improved rights protection: Some first steps and some alternative futures**	**132**
	Towards a new national self-image	133
	Towards Constitutional change	145
	Towards regional autonomy	159
7	**Some conclusions**	**169**
	Bibliography	181
	Index	187

Acknowledgments

With thanks for encouragement and support to Roberto Unger, Russel Barsh, Inge Burgess, Joseph Weiler, Kate Sutherland, Julian Owen, Harold Cardinal, Jason Behrendt (best brother), Raema Behrendt (my beautiful Mum), Paul Behrendt (my Pa), Justice Tony Fitzgerald, Marcia Langton, Bill Jonas, Roberta Sykes, Jilpia Jones, Mona Taylor, Kate Rowe, Dominique Tubier, the staff of the Jumbunna Indigenous House of Learning, and Jo Fox. Special thanks to Kris Faller, Suzy Evans, George Williams, Gordon Hookey, Federation Press (especially Chris Holt) and Geoff Scott.

Chapter 1
Why question the rules?

I was born in 1969, two years after a Constitutional referendum was passed by almost 90 per cent majority of Australians. This referendum allowed Indigenous Australians to be included in the census figures and provided the federal government with the power to make laws in relation to Indigenous people. This was the same year that the policy allowing the removal of Aboriginal children from their families formally ended in New South Wales.

I was born into the generation of Indigenous people who reaped the benefits of the civil rights movement of the 1960s – including greater access to education. I went straight from high school to university, something that previous generations of Indigenous people had never had the opportunity to do.

Despite these changes, I was educated within a school system that taught nothing of Australia's history of the dispossession of its Indigenous people or of the removal of Aboriginal children – historical actions that defined my Indigenous family. As I came to understand my own family history and the story of my grandmother's forced removal from her parents, I became angry that my classmates remained ignorant.

This frustration fuelled my resolve to achieve change through the law. Even as a young adult, I understood the power of the law through its impact on my family — dispossession, removal, incarceration. I became a lawyer to change laws, idealistically to right historical wrongs and make sure that the injustices of the past — the Stolen Generations and land grabs — would not happen again.

I graduated from law school in the year of the *Mabo* case, when a group of Murray Islanders, including Eddie Mabo, sought recognition of their rights over their traditional land. In an historic judgment, the High Court ruled that the Islanders held native title rights over that land, and that the doctrine of *terra nullius*, (literally 'land of no one', declaring that Australia was without prior occupants or sovereigns at the time of European arrival) was false.[1] I was in the middle of my doctoral studies when the *Wik* decision[2] was handed down by the High Court. The *Wik* decision held that native title was not necessarily extinguished by pastoral leases over land, and that both titles could, in fact, co-exist.

What struck me at the time of both decisions was the hostile public reaction to what were, in real terms, minimalist and cautious legal advancements. I was also struck by the subsequent easy ability of legislation to sweep away hard-fought rights recognition. I watched as the rights recognised by the High Court in the *Mabo* and *Wik* cases were extinguished, eroded and/or watered down by the Commonwealth Government.

The willingness of Australian governments to prevent the application of the *Racial Discrimination Act* 1975 (Cth) from protecting Indigenous rights also highlighted the fragility of those rights in Australia.

Prime Minister John Howard's rhetoric surrounding the passing of the *Native Title Amendment Act* 1998 (Cth) brought into focus the conflicting visions Australians have about our country. The Act was a diluted version of a '10 Point Plan' which included:

- reducing the say native title holders have on mineral exploration in their traditional country;
- enabling the States and Territories to replace the right to negotiate on pastoral leases;
- allowing a range of primary production activities to take place on pastoral leases without negotiation with traditional land holders;
- native title holders having less say in a whole range of government activities on their land; and
- making it more difficult for native title holders to present their case in a claims hearing.

When finally passed, the amending legislation reduced the opportunities for native title holders to be consulted about their activities on their traditional land.

In the wake of the *Wik* decision, the Federal Government tried to gain popular support for its proposed legislative changes by

---

1 *Mabo v Queensland (No 2)* (1992) 175 CLR 1.
2 *Wik Peoples v Queensland* (1996) 187 CLR 1.

portraying that pastoral leases were held by small, family-run farms. In reality, many pastoral leases are held by wealthy individuals or corporations. The Prime Minister continued to push an approach informed by the ideologies of white Australian nationalism and a psychological *terra nullius*, playing into 'settlement' myths of Australia's land being tamed by brave men who struggled to make a living off the land (see Chapter 3 for a discussion of nationalism and identity). The Prime Minister stated:

> Australia's farmers, of course, have always occupied a very special place in our heart ... They often endure the heartbreak of drought, the disappointment of bad international prices after a hard-worked season and quite frankly I find it impossible to imagine the Australia I love, without a strong and vibrant farming sector.[3]

This rhetoric sought to appeal to romanticised, nationalistic ideals that ignore the fact that the *Mabo* and *Wik* cases found there was a legitimate property right held by Indigenous peoples; it brushed over the historical context in which dispossession took place. Howard employed a notion of formal equality in this debate: '[W]e have clung tenaciously to the principle that no group in the Australian community should have rights that are not enjoyed by another group.'[4] He also referred to the 'politics of guilt': 'Australians of this generation should not be required to accept the guilt and blame for the past actions and policies over which they had no control.'[5]

Howard's lack of recognition of any historical context regarding the treatment of Aboriginal and Torres Strait Islander people since European settlement — massacres of Indigenous peoples, dispossession, government policies of assimilation and removal of children — enabled him to view the recognition of native title interests in a vacuum.

The Prime Minister claimed that the wrongs committed against Indigenous people were historic and therefore not the responsibility of Australians today. This lack of recognition compounded the continual failure of Australian legal and political institutions to recognise native title as a legitimate property right.

Native title was only recognised legally in 1992 as a result of the *Mabo* judgment and the passing of the *Native Title Act* 1993 by

---

3   'The sooner we get this debate over the better for all of us', *The Age*, 1 December 1997.
4   'Racing towards an election', *Sydney Morning Herald*, 11 April 1998.
5   'Mr Howard unreconciled', *Sydney Morning Herald*, 27 May 1997.

the Keating Government. However, Indigenous dispossession still continues, facilitated by the passing of the *Native Title Amendment Act* 1998 (Cth), the enactment of which limited the circumstances in which native title could be claimed and meant that 80 of the 115 claims then before the Native Title Tribunal in New South Wales (NSW) were dismissed.

The rhetoric employed to stir up antagonism towards native title interests after *Wik* also came into play in the response to the Human Rights and Equal Opportunity Commission (HREOC) report on the activities and legacies of the Aborigines Protection Board. The report contained a detailed look at the experiences of people removed by the Aboriginal welfare regimes in each State and Territory.

The report, *Bringing Them Home*,[6] was released in 1997. It noted the connection between the removal of Indigenous children from their parents – 'the Stolen Generations' – by the State and the problems with suicide, mental illness, substance abuse, family breakdown and cyclical poverty in Indigenous communities. Despite Federal Government attempts to minimise and quantify the effect of the removal policy, Aboriginal people in NSW attest to the fact that there is not an Aboriginal family in that State that was not adversely affected by this policy in some way.

Before the HREOC report brought the matter to the attention of the nation, very few Australians knew of the existence of the government's Aboriginal child removal policy. Many Australians felt moved by the revelations of the report, including Governor-General William Deane who stated: 'It is vital that we acknowledge past injustices and recognise wounds inflicted in our earlier policy of denial.'[7]

However, a different response came from Australians who embrace the Australian identity only in its colonial manifestation. This response was reflected in John Howard's assertion that Australians should feel neither guilt nor responsibility for past actions and policies. Nowhere was this philosophy more evident than in the Federal Government submission to the Senate Legal and Constitutional References Committee on the 'Inquiry into the Stolen Generation.' In that submission, the government stated:

---

6 Human Rights and Equal Opportunity Commission (HREOC), 1997, *Bringing Them Home: A Guide to the Findings and Recommendations of the National Inquiry into the Separation of Aboriginal and Torres Strait Islander Children from their Families*, Australian Government Publishing Service.

7 'Governor joins call for apology', *Sydney Morning Herald*, 3 June 1997.

WHY QUESTION THE RULES?

- 'There was never a "generation" of stolen children'; and
- 'Emotional reaction to heart-wrenching stories is understandable, but it is impossible to evaluate by contemporary standards decisions that were taken in the past.'

Ironically, it appears it is often easier for Australians to see the context and legacies of conflicts in other countries rather than in their own. For example, it is more readily acknowledged by Australians that violent conflict in Northern Ireland or the former Yugoslavia is complicated by competing passions steeped in a complex historical background. Australians can see the disadvantages faced by African-Americans and readily understand their contemporary situation as a legacy of slavery, but it seems harder to make the connection between historical actions and contemporary realities as they have played out on their own soil. The connection between past and present seems to be a difficult conceptual leap, even when the links have been set out clearly in thoughtful, well-researched reports such as those by the Royal Commission into Aboriginal Deaths in Custody (RCIADIC),[8] which examined the alarming high mortality rates of Indigenous prisoners, and the HREOC report on the Stolen Generations.

The 'politics of guilt' is often used as a way to distance Australians from their past and prevents meaningful interaction with an understanding of Australian history and Australian identity. In fact, those who claim that the mistakes and injustices in Australia's history should be ignored (because they supposedly generate guilt) make two mistakes.

- They minimise the efforts and contributions of those Australians — black and white — who have sought to improve the situation of all Australians, and who have worked to counter prejudice and discrimination.
- They ignore the fact that confronting history, especially the moments that might not make one proud, allows the legacies of those moments to be countered. It is not about shaming or 'guilting' or blaming. It is about acknowledging a truth, and with that acknowledgment will come reconciliation, healing, empowerment and pride.

---

8   Royal Commission into Aboriginal Deaths in Custody, 1991, *National Report: Overview and Recommendations*, Australian Government Publishing Service.

The populist appeal of Howard's romanticised, nationalistic, simplistic and erroneous account of Australian history, and his blind denial of historical facts and their legacies, raises a very difficult question for me as a lawyer, as an Aboriginal person and as someone who believes in protecting basic rights: How can the hard-fought recognition of rights achieved in the *Mabo* case and the *Wik* case be protected from being overturned or eroded by the legislature, the popularly-elected branch of our government?

This issue becomes especially pertinent given the remaining ambiguity of the decision in the *Hindmarsh Island Bridge* case.[9] This was a case where the Ngarrindjeri women in South Australia challenged the *Hindmarsh Island Bridge Act* 1997 (Cth). The Act prevented the plaintiffs from claiming that the area had secret and sacred significance to them and denied them the use of heritage protection legislation.[10] The case has left a question mark over whether the 'race power' contained in s 51(xxvi) of the Australian Constitution empowers the government to make laws to the detriment of Indigenous Australians.

Two matters become self-evidently crucial.

- The importance of removing historical ignorance surrounding the experiences and situation of Indigenous Australians, including reconciling Australians with their history and understanding the way historical acts leave contemporary legacies.
- Creating a concrete rights framework that will protect the basic rights of *all* Australians, especially those of one of the most vulnerable groups in Australian society, the Indigenous community.

While understanding that these are two key elements in the step towards the protection of Indigenous rights, it is important to appreciate that several other issues also need to be addressed. If piecemeal legislative changes and sporadic court decisions are failing to produce an Australia that treats all its citizens fairly, other strategic approaches need to be considered that will create *substantive changes* to the situation of all Australians, especially the most economically, socially and legally vulnerable.

---

9   *Kartinyeri v Commonwealth* (1998) 152 ALR 540.
10 For a concise brief of the *Hindmarsh Island Bridge* case, see T Blackshield, M Coper and G Williams, *The Oxford Companion to the High Court*, Oxford University Press, p 325.

WHY QUESTION THE RULES?

Australians and the first Australians

The relationship of non-Indigenous Australians to Indigenous peoples continues to be a problematic one. From periods of cultural genocidal practices – invasion, massacres of Aboriginal people, the removal of Aboriginal children from their families – to theft of property and denial of fundamental rights, it is a relationship complicated by historical injustice, compounded by institutional legacies and an idealised nationalism.

Today, over 30 years after the 1967 Constitutional amendment, Indigenous people are still the most socio-economically disadvantaged within Australian society and are still vulnerable to systemic discriminatory practices. Indigenous Australians continue to be the poorest sector of the Australian community.

In many respects, Indigenous Australia is a typical profile of a conquered and colonised people and at just over 2 per cent of the population, are an impoverished minority.

To provide a snap-shot from the 1990s:

- The life expectancy of Aboriginal people is 20-21 years less than the general population.
- Aborigines and Torres Strait Islanders are more than four times as likely to die as non-Aboriginal people if less than 30, and seven times more likely to die (if over 30).
- Indigenous childhood mortality is still more than three to five times higher than that for other Australian children.
- Infectious diseases are 12 times higher than the Australian average.
- Diabetes affects 30 per cent of people in Aboriginal and Torres Strait Islander communities.
- Hospital admissions for Aboriginal men are 71 per cent higher and for Aboriginal women are 57 per cent higher than for non-Aboriginal men and women.
- 13.6 per cent of Indigenous people have tertiary degrees, compared with 34.4 per cent of all Australians.
- The unemployment rate is 22.7 per cent for Indigenous people, compared with 9.2 per cent for the general population.
- 30.8 per cent of Indigenous households owned or were purchasing their lands, compared with 70 per cent of all Australians.

- The mean individual Indigenous income is 65 per cent of that of the general population.
- Indigenous peoples are 17.3 times more likely to be arrested; 14.7 times more likely to be imprisoned; and 16.5 times more likely to die in custody than non-Indigenous Australians.[11]

These statistics highlight the undeniable socio-economic disparity between Indigenous people and other Australians in every measurable service sector: access to medical treatment, education, employment and economic development. The processes of dispossession and colonisation have placed Australia's Indigenous community in a cycle of poverty: poor health, little education, high rates of unemployment, low incomes and poor access to essential services. It is perhaps the biggest condemnation that many of these disparities occur in areas that are considered to be unquestioned rights for other Australians.

Unable to form a political majority, Indigenous Australians have had to rely on an unresponsive court system and the wavering sympathies of the Australian community in order to have their basic rights recognised and protected.

Indigenous Australia remains the unreconciled, unattended aspect of Australia's past and present and until this relationship has been attended to and reconciled, it will continue to divide Australians.

Redefining the relationship between Indigenous and non-Indigenous Australians is a challenge that involves assessing the impact of historical injustice. It is only when we understand how the ideologies of colonialism have permeated today's institutions that we can begin to break the grip of the historical legacy. Once that grip is broken, Australians will be free to explore alternatives to colonisation and assimilation.

Nowhere is this historic, institutional legacy more apparent — and perhaps most symbolic — than in the Australian Constitution, a document drafted with the erroneous assumption that Indigenous

---

11 Sources: Aboriginal and Torres Strait Islander Commission, 1999, *Indigenous Australians Today*, Aboriginal and Torres Strait Islander Commission; Australian Bureau of Statistics, *Australia Now – Australia Social Trends 2002: Health, Habitat and Morbidity: Mortality of Aboriginal and Torres Strait Islander Peoples* <www.abs.gov.au> accessed 20 January 2003; Federal Race Discrimination Commissioner, 1997, *Face the Facts*, Federal Race Discrimination Commissioner.

people were a dying race, and guided by the offensive principle that it was acceptable to discriminate on the basis of race.

While the recognition of past injustices will make a symbolic atonement for the misdeeds of colonisation, there needs to be a concerted, strategic campaign to transform the institutions within Australia that have entrenched ideologies that operate to exclude Indigenous people. This needs to be coupled with the creation of opportunities and arrangements that empower Indigenous people, allowing them to transcend the socio-economic circumstances into which they are born.

Practical reconciliation or the rights agenda?

The approach taken to dealing with the socio-economic disparities between Indigenous Australians and the general populace has become fractured. There are two answers often proposed as the solution:

- A welfare approach to breaking the cycle of poverty by injecting funds into the areas of need, an approach sometimes referred to as 'practical reconciliation'.
- A rights framework that focuses on altering the institutions which continue the colonisation process.

There is a tension between the concept of practical reconciliation and the development of mechanisms that protect recognised human rights, that is, a rights framework. While the link between economic issues and rights issues is not being made, the notion of practical reconciliation is antagonistic to a broader rights framework because practical reconciliation is only a set of policies that react to emerging problems, and in doing so ignores the longer-term structural and institutional changes that can protect rights. This book proposes the need to take a new approach to the connection between broader legal reforms and economic development, one that moves away from a welfare mentality.

This book considers why a rights framework is important by examining what it can achieve. It seeks to address some of the concerns about a big picture approach achieving a more equitable and just society through constitutional, legislative and jurisprudential change.

In 2000, at the hand-over of the Final Report by the Council for Aboriginal Reconciliation (set up by the previous Labor Government in September 1991), Prime Minister John Howard announced that his government rejected the Report's recommendation of a treaty between Australian and Indigenous peoples, preferring instead to concentrate on the concept of practical reconciliation. Practical reconciliation describes a policy of government funding in targeted areas that go to the core of socio-economic disadvantage, namely, employment, education, housing and health. Howard said in his address at the presentation of the Final Report:

> We are determined to design policy and structure administrative arrangements to address these very real issues and ensure standards in education and employment, health and housing improve to a significant degree ... That is why we place a great deal of emphasis on practical reconciliation.[12]

Howard pointed to the amount of dollars his government had spent on 'Indigenous-specific programs'.

> A measure of the genuineness of the government's commitment to practical reconciliation is that the $2.3 billion now annually spent on Indigenous-specific programmes is, in real terms, a record for any government — Coalition or Labor.[13]

What Howard didn't detail in his address is that part of that $2.3 billion went towards defending the Stolen Generations test case brought by Peter Gunner and Lorna Cabillo in the Northern Territory[14] (in which the plaintiffs sought to claim damages for the emotional and physical harms they suffered while removed from their families) and were also directed into the various government arms that were actively trying to defeat native title claims. In other words, money spent preventing the recognition and protection of Indigenous rights was counted as money allocated for specific policy areas of practical reconciliation.

Practical reconciliation aims to resolve the legacies of colonisation by focusing on relieving socio-economic disparity. In his Menzies Lecture, delivered on 13 December 2000, just a few days after receiving the Final Report from the Council for Aboriginal Reconciliation, Howard said:

---

12 J Howard, 2000b, Address at the presentation of the Final Report to Federal Parliament by the Council for Aboriginal Reconciliation, 7 December, p 3.
13 Howard, 2000b, p 3.
14 *Cubillo v Commonwealth* (2000) 174 ALR 97.

WHY QUESTION THE RULES?

It is true, as was noted recently, that past policies designed to assist have often failed to recognise the significance of indigenous culture and resulted in the further marginalisation of Aboriginal and Torres Strait Islander people from the social, cultural and economic development of mainstream Australian society.[15]

Looked at this way, the current socio-economic disparity is the result of past cultural conflict and unsympathetic policy-making and it is what has been instrumental in establishing a welfare mentality. According to Howard, 'This led to a culture of dependency and victimhood, which condemned many Indigenous Australians to lives of poverty and further devalued their culture in the eyes of their fellow Australians'.[16]

In Howard's view, the main issues are dependency, victimhood and poverty; according to the advocates of practical reconciliation, these can be redressed by a more benevolent legislature.

It is absolutely true that past government policies such as child removal practices have contributed to the socio-economic inequalities and systemic racism experienced in Indigenous communities and families today. But as the *Kruger* case (the first Stolen Generations case to be brought before the High Court) illustrated,[17] this has been compounded by the absence of a rights framework that can prevent unfair and racist policy-making.

For a government who claims that Indigenous problems should not just have money thrown at them, its focus on the amount of dollars spent – without analysing whether those dollars actually benefit Indigenous people and communities – is ironic. By not being concerned with broader, long-term, structural goals, it confines its activities to reactive policy-making.

Practical reconciliation does not attack the systemic and institutionalised aspects of the impediments to socio-economic development. While claiming that 'more handouts' are not going to make a difference, the government fails to address the issues and put strategies in place that go to the heart of historical and institutional racism. This approach also fails to understand that there needs to be tangible protection of rights, including economic and property rights. The

---

15 J Howard, 2000c, *Menzies Lecture Series: Perspectives on Aboriginal and Torres Strait Islander Issues*, 13 December, p 3.
16 Howard, 2000c, p 3.
17 *Kruger v Commonwealth* (1997) 190 CLR 1.

recognition and protection of these rights would put land under people's feet, allow access to natural and other economic resources and work towards ensuring that Indigenous communities were economically self-sufficient.

Without a working rights framework, there is no ability to create and protect the rights to economic self-sufficiency.

In recent times, there has been an emerging voice from some members of Indigenous communities questioning the emphasis on the need for a rights framework, with particular frustration expressed at the slowness of the process. Their claim, that esoteric talk of constitutional change does not put food on the table or end high levels of violence in the community, is compelling. It is easy, when placed in that light, to dismiss the focus on the rights agenda as the privilege of the elite.

Granted, structural change, particularly constitutional change, is a long-term goal. However, there are several things that the rights agenda offers Indigenous people, even in the short term.

First, a rights framework provides a language with which to communicate about harms suffered and political aspirations. The existence of an agreed standard of rights creates a medium through which to communicate harms suffered. For example, the plaintiffs in *Kruger* were able to articulate the harms suffered by those affected by the child removal policy and, in particular, were able to show that these are rights that others take for granted, such as freedom of movement and due process before the law.

In a more positive way, the language of rights can provide a means of communicating political aspirations: the right to hunt and fish, the right to native title, the right to work, the right to provide for one's family, the right to education, the right to adequate health services.

Secondly, the existing international rights framework provides minimum standards against which the federal government can be held accountable, and provides a basis for objective assessment of the recognition and protection of Indigenous rights. This objective assessment was particularly evident in the 2000 report by the United Nations' Committee on the Elimination of all forms of Racial Discrimination, which was critical of Australia's record.[18] It found that the Australian government had failed to meet certain obligations that it

---

18 CERD/C/56/Misc42/rev3, 2000.

had agreed to uphold under the *Convention to Eliminate all forms of Racial Discrimination* (CERD). The CERD Committee's report expressed concern about the absence of any entrenched law guaranteeing against racial discrimination, provisions of the *Native Title Amendment Act* 1998 (Cth), the failure to apologise for the Stolen Generations and the Federal Government's refusal to interfere to change the mandatory sentencing laws operational in both the Northern Territory and Western Australia. The need for objective international standards is particularly necessary while Australia is without domestic rights protection.

Thirdly, a rights framework can also offer long-term solutions that should not be dismissed because of the length of time needed for its implementation. Such a rights framework can provide renewed protection of Indigenous rights and substantially change the status quo between Indigenous peoples and the Australian state. Such institutional change needs to be targeted at the Constitution, since it is the document that establishes government and, not insignificantly, symbolises our coming together to consent to nationhood.

Grass roots issues that affect Indigenous people day-to-day — violence against women, child sexual abuse, systemic poverty, lack of access to services, substance abuse, high youth suicide rates — are issues that need to be addressed as a priority, but this needs to be done in conjunction with, not in the absence of, a broader framework for institutional change. The objectives of this book are to explain *why* and to show *how* that can be done.

A belief in substantive equality

The 1967 Referendum was a symbolic act of recognition that raised Indigenous expectations for the beginning of a new, inclusive relationship in which Indigenous peoples would enjoy, on the face of it, the same rights and protections as all Australians. It was not the first time that Indigenous people had sought symbolic inclusion with the hope that *neutral, formal equality* would lead to an improvement in circumstance and treatment.

However, since the 1967 Referendum, it has become increasingly evident that the formal structures and institutions within Australia have not changed enough to equalise — let alone reverse — the socio-economic impact of colonisation and past government policies and practices.

At the same time that momentum gathered for the 1967 Referendum, Aboriginal and Torres Strait Islander people began to push even harder for the recognition of their traditional property rights and assertion of sovereignty. This protest led to the establishment in 1972 of an Aboriginal Tent Embassy on the lawn of Parliament House in Canberra. There were two strains of political strategy being used by Indigenous people at the Tent Embassy that were integral to Indigenous people's aspirations that on the first appearance might have seemed contradictory.

- Indigenous people wanted to be treated equally with all other Australians and demanded the reversal of paternalistic, racist and discriminatory practices. The poverty and historical treatment of Indigenous Australians emphasised the fact that they did not enjoy the same access to society and the same rights as other Australians.
- The notion of a Tent Embassy highlighted the fact that Indigenous people saw themselves as a distinct people, a distinct nation and a political entity.

On the one hand, Aboriginal people were claiming *equality within* the Australian state. On the other, they were defining themselves as a *separate entity*, questioning the legality of Australian institutions to rule over their lives. These seemingly paradoxical claims require further investigation. In understanding how these claims of inclusion and difference co-exist, the political agenda of Indigenous peoples is revealed to be rich and complex rather than confused and contradictory. This complexity reveals the intricate relationship between claims of equal protection and special protection. The investigation here into the political aspirations of the Indigenous community for the protection of rights will consider the way that seemingly contradictory aspirations can actually work together to produce a more comprehensive and representative process of protecting rights.

More than a 'noisy minority': The democratic challenge posed by Indigenous people

It is a mistake to think of Indigenous rights and well-being as merely an 'Indigenous issue' or 'Indigenous problem'. The rights and quality of life for Aboriginal and Torres Strait Islander communities pose questions and have implications for Australian society as a whole, and their

WHY QUESTION THE RULES?

current situation offers a challenge to all Australians – especially jurists, rights advocates and the political elite of Australian communities.

The situation demands consideration of socio-economic equality, the importance of inclusion and political and cultural recognition. The challenge of improving rights protections needs to be approached by broader strategies than piecemeal court wins and band-aid welfare measures. Finding a better approach to the protection of Indigenous rights is a multi-faceted process that must include the following.

- A better understanding of how inequalities have become institutionalised, allowing 'formal equality' to become a tool that maintains an unequal *status quo* and perpetuates injustice. How can seemingly neutral laws operate to produce inequality? For example, how does property law, seemingly neutral, perpetuate a disadvantage that leaves Indigenous people continually dispossessed?
- A thorough understanding of what Indigenous political aspirations are and an exploration of how those aspirations can be accommodated within Australia's institutions. This includes aspirations of framework agreements and/or a treaty.
- A coupling of legal victories with attempts to change public (mis)perceptions about Indigenous Australians. These changes need to be undertaken in concert with changes to Australia's institutions. What kind of Australia do we want to be? How do we see ourselves?
- An exploration and implementation of the ideals of identity and equality and Indigenous legal and political aspirations through changes to Australia's institutions. Such institutional changes need to aim at making institutions more effective at achieving equality and fairness in their operations.

This final point — the need for institutional change — highlights a very important issue. If Australia's institutions cannot protect one of the most vulnerable sectors of the Australian community, how democratic are they? Do they embody the ideals we have as a nation if they produce and compound injustice and inequity? It is in answering this question that Indigenous rights take on a special role: they are the litmus test of how well our institutions operate and of how fair and equal our society is. As former Prime Minister Gough Whitlam once said: 'Australia's treatment of her Aboriginal people will be the thing upon which the rest of the world will judge Australia and Australians — not just now, but in the greater perspective of history.'[19]

The directions and solutions to the dilemmas facing Aboriginal and Torres Strait Islander people and communities have wider implications since the institutional form given to the recognition of Indigenous rights and Australian democratic ideals will shape the kind of society that Australia will be. For this reason, these institutional goals should be guided by a vision of the kind of society we all want to live in, a process that would make institutions more responsive and beneficial for all Australians. It is a process that sees Indigenous Australians as the litmus test of success, rather than the exception to the rule. As part of the process of assessing the effectiveness of Australia's laws and institutions in protecting the rights of Indigenous peoples, the socio-economic results they produce should be objectively assessed against notions of democracy that reflect the ideals that Australian society should embody. This moves away from treating Indigenous rights as an Indigenous 'problem' that needs to be solved and instead treats it as an issue whose resolution will benefit *all* Australians by virtue of improved institutions, service delivery and rights protection. It also takes Indigenous people from the periphery of debates about rights, politics and ideals and places them in the middle of those discussions.

A concept of democracy

Democracy, the label given to the idea that a system of government that is fair and inclusive, is an amorphous concept and needs to be defined by the visions and ideals of the kind of Australia we want to live in. John Dewey provides the following useful definition.

> From the standpoint of the individual, it consists in having a responsible share according to capacity in forming and directing the activities of the groups to which one belongs and in particular according to need in the values which the groups sustain. From the standpoint of the groups, it demands liberation of the potentialities of members of a group in harmony with the interests and goods which are common. Since every individual is a member of many groups, this specification cannot be fulfilled except when different groups interact flexibly and fully in connection with other groups.[20]

---

19 Cited in H Reynolds, 1992, *The Law of the Land*, Penguin, p 183.
20 J Dewey, 1991 (orig 1923), *The Public and Its Problems*, Swallow, p 147.

WHY QUESTION THE RULES?

Dewey's definition identifies certain cornerstones of 'democracy'. He notes:

- the importance of the integrity and autonomy of the individual;
- the importance of the ability of the individual to participate in associations that form the quality of his other life;
- the difficulty in balancing the interests of *individuals* with the interests of *groups*; and
- the need to achieve democracy with flexibility and that such flexibility must be present in the institutions created to achieve democratic ideals.

The complex relationship of individual freedom to group identity is a backdrop for universal questions raised by the issues related to the protection of Indigenous rights regarding the institutional framework in all (democratic) societies:

- To what extent should institutions recognise group rights and rights to association?
- What institutions should we use to structure these societies?
- How can institutions allow individual freedom?

All societies grapple with tensions over what values should be protected. In trying to find alternative paths for the improved protection of Indigenous rights, the following needs to be considered:

- the relationship of the individual to their cultural and political groups;
- institutional arrangements which could reflect that relationship.

There are two issues wrapped up in the above questions.

- Indigenous identity: What is it? How should it be preserved?
- How should that identity be given institutional recognition? How can institutions give substantive content to rights?

Roberto Mangabiera Unger of Harvard Law School adds another dimension to this conception of democracy when he stresses that it should be understood as:

> the effort to make a practical and moral success of society by reconciling the pursuit of two families of goods: the good of material progress, liberating us from the drudgery and incapacity and

giving arms and wings to our desires, and the good of individual emancipation, freeing us from the grinding schemes of social division and hierarchy.[21]

Unger stresses two elements:

- the importance of economic development;
- the importance of individual freedom.

These two elements need to guide any attempt at developing a framework for Indigenous rights. Australia's Indigenous population, a small, impoverished, minority is in need of effective and innovative solutions to socio-economic and political challenges in the face of an unsympathetic public and a hostile government.

New approaches to Indigenous rights protection

By exploring the extent of Indigenous visions of equality, inclusion and autonomy, a reconceptualisation of approaches to the better protection of Indigenous rights should occur. This means, as a start, exploring what Indigenous political aspirations encompass. What is it that Indigenous people need? The public dialogue with (rather than about) Aboriginal people is a recent approach to policy-making concerning Indigenous issues, so it is not surprising that many non-Indigenous people are not familiar with the political aspirations of Indigenous people and their communities.

In Indigenous expression of political aspirations, two political goals seems ubiquitous: the claims for the recognition of 'Aboriginal sovereignty' and 'self-determination'. The key to understanding the Indigenous political agenda is to unlock what it is that Aboriginal people are describing when employing the terms 'Aboriginal sovereignty' and 'self-determination'.

A deconstruction of these terms reveals a different political agenda from 'sovereignty' as it is used in an international legal context. 'Sovereignty' and 'self-determination' need to be defined in this context so that the proper parameters of the rights debates in Australia can be established to complement and facilitate the exact rights that Indigenous people are seeking. It is here that the complexity of political terms can be deconstructed and the co-existence of

---

21 R Unger, 1996, *What Should Legal Analysis Become?*, Verso, p 6.

WHY QUESTION THE RULES?

seemingly conflicting agendas reconciled; autonomy within the state coupled with inclusion through substantive equality; respect for individual identity in tandem with the protection of group identity.

Once the rights sought by Indigenous people have been articulated, ways of recognising Indigenous aspirations become the next challenge. It is therefore necessary to look at what is contained within these claims of 'sovereignty' and 'self-determination' and then, from this deconstruction, to develop experimental democratic programs that will assist in making those aspirations realisable.

From a deciphering of the claims to 'Aboriginal sovereignty', it becomes apparent not only that many of the international implications of the term are absent but that many of the elements that are seen to be included in the claim are also rights that should *already* be protected and recognised under existing Australian law. They are rights that are recognised as fundamental either within Australian law or within international instruments ratified by Australia.

It is here again that the lesson learnt from the Tent Embassy should be reiterated: a program of piecemeal, episodic changes have not taken Indigenous people forward to the stage where they enjoy the same rights as other Australians. Another approach, one that challenges the institutions of Australian society and their entrenched biases, needs to be examined. Strategies for the better protection of Indigenous rights must seek to implement a process of institutional change and, in order to achieve this, it is necessary to expose and erode the dominant, seemingly neutral, ideological base of institutional frameworks. Without an accompanying project of institutional change, Indigenous Australians will be frustrated with the critique and left wanting for practical outcomes and the achievement of visionary aims.

◆ ◆ ◆

Beginning with an exploration of the way in which seemingly neutral laws have contributed to the erosion of the rights of Indigenous Australians, this book calls into question the notion of formal equality as a determinant of fairness. This leads to an investigation and deconstruction of Australia's idealised nationalist identity that can still be acknowledged as informing decision-making processes and institutions, to the detriment of those who challenge those values. At the same time, it identifies the importance of identity and the sense of self. Questioning these assumptions leads to the need to create a new perspective from which to start thinking about institutional change that might better promote fairness within Australian society for Indigenous people.

This book then considers a spectrum of what it is that Indigenous people aspire to politically under the rubric of 'Aboriginal sovereignty' and 'self-determination'. This is not meant to be a definitive exploration, merely a chance to get a sense of the scope of Indigenous political goals. It will also enable an assessment of the democratic principles missing from Australia's institutions, and examine a program for institutional change that will inject those values into our societal institutions and structures.

Following from this, the book explores what can be seen as *some* of the key steps necessary to shift the historical legacies and contemporary experiences and improve Australia's institutions for Indigenous Australians — and all Australians. The purpose is not to state definitively the Indigenous political agenda nor to provide answers to what should be done. Rather, this book seeks to inject the current debates with some possible options, bringing attention to the inherent inequities within the system and highlighting the pervasiveness of Australia's psychological *terra nullius*.

Chapter 2

The myth of law's neutrality: Why formal equality doesn't work

Fairness, equality and justice in Australia are often asserted as being achievable through the principle of 'one law for all'. This notion of formal equality is, however, problematic in practice. I want to use three examples to illustrate the falsity of the claim that laws in Australia have been applied neutrally.

Australia's laws on mandatory sentencing provide evidence of the way in which a neutral law can have a disproportionate impact on particular members of the community. The Constitution acts as an example of how a seemingly non-discriminatory document can be infused with ideology in a manner that can have real and detrimental consequences to vulnerable sectors of the society it regulates.

A deconstruction of Australia's property laws offers an example of how the ideologies rooted in Australia's nationalism permeate and shape laws and institutions.

This examination argues that seemingly neutral institutions are actually charged with colonial ideologies, legacies and a psychological *terra nullius* that cause disparate outcomes, with the result that 'special laws' are anything but beneficial. Together, these three examples demonstrate that laws can appear to be neutral, or even beneficial, but can have a disproportionate impact on particular sectors of the community.

Different conceptions of justice

Same law, disparate outcomes: Mandatory sentencing schemes

The statistics relating to Indigenous people's contact with the criminal justice system tells a story of over-representation. At just on 2 per cent of the overall Australian population,[1] Indigenous people including men, women and juveniles, make up 28.6 per cent of the prison population.[2] At the time of the RCIADIC established in October 1987, Aboriginal people were 20 times more likely than a non-Aboriginal person to die in custody. Today, they are 26 times more likely to die in custody than non-Aboriginal people. Statistics indicate that one in seven Aboriginal people are in jail;[3] and one in four Indigenous men are in jail. Among Indigenous Australians 13 years and over, one in five had been arrested in the last five years.[4] Latest figures are even higher, despite the RCIADIC and its recommendations.

---

1   The 1996 census counted 386,000, an increase of 40,700 since 1991. It represents 2.1% of the total Australian population (18,310,700) This census also showed an increase in the number of people who identified themselves as Indigenous. Australian Bureau of Statistics, *Estimates of Aboriginal and Torres Strait Islander Populations* <www.abs.gov.au/Austats/>, accessed 20 January 2003.

2   H McRae, G Nettheim and L Beacroft, 1991, *Aboriginal Legal Issues: Commentary and Materials*, Law Book, p 242. A 1996 report released by the Minister of Corrective Services (NSW) showed that the representation of Aborigines as a proportion of the State's prison population had climbed from 8.5 per cent in 1982 to 12.4 per cent. The report noted that there were more men in NSW prisons than there were in universities: 'Jail shake-up keeps blacks out of cells', *Sydney Morning Herald*, 19 November 1996.

3   Aboriginal and Torres Strait Islander Commission, 1995, *Annual Report 1994–1995*, Australian Government Publishing Service, p 129; J Behrendt and L Behrendt, 'Aboriginal Deaths in Custody Since the Royal Commission', 2(59) *Aboriginal Law Bulletin* 4 (December 1992).

4   R Madden, 1995, *National Aboriginal and Torres Strait Islander Survey, 1994*, Australian Bureau of Statistics, p 59.

Trudy Harris reported that: 'Aboriginal juvenile imprisonments have reached 'astronomical' levels with black convicts amounting for more than one in three jail inmates ... Aborigines aged 10 to 14 are 33 times more likely to be in detention than other juveniles of the same age ...' Harris also noted that the Convention of the Rights of the Child states that detention for juveniles should only be used as a last resort: T Harris, 1996, 'One in three jailed juveniles Aboriginal', *The Weekend Australian*, 26–27 October, p 8.

Amnesty International has criticised Queensland police practices. In one instance, police took three Aboriginal boys, aged 12 to 14, to an industrial wasteland 14 kilometres from Brisbane to 'reflect on their misdemeanours': see C Skehan, 1997, 'Amnesty targets law in Report', *Sydney Morning Herald*, 19 June.

THE MYTH OF LAW'S NEUTRALITY

The majority of the contact between Indigenous people and the law occurs in interactions with the police. This has an historical context, since it was law enforcement officers that led the massacres of Aboriginal people from early settlement up until the 1930s and implemented the removals policy in force until 1967 – that is, it was the police who came to take children away from their families.

Australian police are, generally, from the non-Indigenous community and many of them believe stereotypes perpetuated about Indigenous people (for example, that Aboriginal people are drunkards; that they are prone to commit crime; that they are unemployed and unemployable; that Aboriginal women are bad mothers). There is a high level of tolerance within the police force of racism towards Indigenous people by police officers. Armed with the negative stereotypes generated by Australian popular culture about Indigenous people, they exacerbate problems by targeting and over-policing Aboriginal populations. Indigenous people are more likely to be arrested for a summary offence than a non-Aboriginal person.[5]

Arresting a person for a summary offence such as drunken behaviour or offensive language is a discretionary action. The rules may be set but there is a great deal of discretion available to law enforcement officers as to how those rules will be applied – when they determine who they will arrest or who they will let off with a warning and when they decide what charges, if any, will be laid. It is this discretion, and any bias or prejudice within that decision-making process, that will impact on the way these rules will be applied. At the time of the RCIADIC, 57 per cent of Aboriginal people in police custody were detained for drunkenness, while only 27 per cent of non-Aboriginal people were held for the same offence.[6] Aboriginal people were detained for twice as long as non-Aboriginal people.[7] One survey reported that in the previous 12 months, one in ten Aboriginal men reported being harassed by the police.[8]

Discretionary implementation is also apparent when the judiciary decide how an offender will be punished and what length any prison term will be. The problems with bias and prejudice within the

---

5   C Cunneen and T Libesman, *Indigenous People and the Law*, Butterworths, 1995, p 60.
6   Royal Commission into Aboriginal Deaths in Custody, 1991, p 228.
7   Royal Commission into Aboriginal Deaths in Custody, 1991, p 288.
8   Madden, 1995, p 59.

decision-making processes of the criminal justice system were identified by the RCIADIC as part of the factors leading to the over-representation of Indigenous people in the criminal justice system.[9]

Ironically, mandatory sentencing schemes take away the judiciary's discretion, and they do so absolutely. Mandatory sentencing schemes were introduced in Western Australia and the Northern Territory in 1996 (subsequently repealed in the Northern Territory by the Labor Government elected in 2001).

The schemes thus fail to deliver a just outcome by prohibiting the judiciary from considering mitigating factors or issuing alternative punishments to incarceration that may be more appropriate. These schemes prescribe the sentences that judges are to impose on offenders convicted of certain property offences, such as criminal damage and receiving stolen goods (for example, 14 days for a first offence, 90 days for a second offence and one year for a third offence). By dictating to members of the judiciary the sentences that are to be imposed, mandatory sentencing violates the principle that sentences should be in proportion to the seriousness of the offence. The following two cases bear this out.

- An 18-year-old Indigenous man obeyed his father and admitted to police that he stole a $2.50 cigarette lighter. He was sentenced to 14 days in prison.
- A 29-year-old homeless Indigenous man wandered into a backyard when drunk and took a $15 towel. It was his third minor property offence. He was imprisoned for one year.[10]

Mandatory sentencing also ignores recommendations in reports and by experts that, especially for juveniles and first offenders, detention should be an option of last resort. It not only undermines the independence and discretion of the judiciary by dictating aspects of the judicial-making process, it also imposes arbitrary sentences on offenders.[11] The provisions upon which mandatory sentencing is based focus on the punitive and retributive roles of the criminal

---

9 Commissioner Hal Wootten, 1898, Report of the Inquiry into the Death of Malcolm Charles Smith, AGPS, p 87.
10 Human Rights and Equal Opportunity Commission (HREOC), 1999, Social Justice Report 1999, Human Rights and Equal Opportunity Commission, p 95.
11 J McCulloch,' Mandatory Sentencing: Creating an Incarcerated Generation', 47 (June-July 2000) Arena Magazine, p 33.

justice system rather than on the rehabilitative and reformative functions.[12] Nor do such provisions seek to address the underlying causes of the offending behaviour.

If mandatory sentencing may seem to be neutral in that it prescribes the same sentences in the legislation for crimes regardless of who perpetrates them, its supposed fairness masks the fact that this prescription places increased greater discretion and power in the hands of the police and prosecutors who decide who will be charged and with what. Unlike members of the bench, who have to make their judgments public, law enforcement officers do not have to provide reasons for their decisions.

There is another inherent inequality within this kind of legislative scheme. By focusing on the property offences most commonly committed by disadvantaged groups – such as the poor, the homeless, women and Indigenous people – mandatory sentencing discriminates against the poorest sectors of the community. The legislation does not target property offences such as fraud or insider trading that are committed by more affluent persons (and which arguably cause greater social and economic harm). Since Indigenous people are amongst the poorest members of the community and are more likely than non-Indigenous people to be homeless, unemployed, dependant on welfare or have no income at all, this makes them more likely to commit the offences covered by the legislation.[13]

The Human Rights and Equal Opportunity Commission's *Social Justice Report 1999* presented alarming statistics concerning Indigenous juvenile incarceration as a result of mandatory sentencing schemes.[14] According to the report, rates of over-representation of Indigenous youth in the criminal justice system were increasing.

- In 1993, an Indigenous youth was 17 more times likely to be detained in custody than a non-Indigenous youth. By 1996, this rate had increased so that an Indigenous youth was 21 more times likely to be detained in custody than a non-Indigenous youth.
- Between June 1994 and June 1997, there was a 20 per cent increase in the number of young Indigenous people in detention. The

---

12 See D Roche, 1999, *Mandatory Sentencing*, Trends and Issues in Crime and Criminal Justice No 138, Australian Institute of Criminology, p 2.
13 McCulloch, p 34.
14 HREOC, 1999, p 92.

correlative level of over-representation for that period increased from 18.9 per cent in 1994 to 24.61 per cent in 1997.[15]

Statistics for the June 1999 quarter for the two jurisdictions with mandatory sentencing schemes (NT and WA) indicate that 76 per cent of all prisoners in the Northern Territory and 34 per cent of all prisoners in Western Australia were Indigenous.

HREOC noted that even though on the face of it the legislation may not seem discriminatory, 'where a pattern of sentencing reveals that certain groups of children are more likely to receive the harshest penalties, sentencing is suspect.'[16]

The impact of mandatory sentencing laws on Indigenous women has been particularly harsh, with estimates based on figures from the Northern Territory Correctional Services Department of 'a 223% increase in the number of Indigenous women incarcerated in the first year of operation of the legislation. As of 30 June 1999, Indigenous women made up 91% of all women prisoners.'[17]

On 24 March 2000, the Committee on the Elimination of Racial Discrimination issued a report critical of the Howard Government's record on human rights protected under the *Convention on the Elimination of all forms of Racial Discrimination* (CERD). In particular, the concluding observations by the Committee included expressions of concern over the 'mandatory sentencing schemes which target offences committed disproportionately by Indigenous Australians, especially juveniles, creating a racially discriminatory impact on already high rates of Indigenous incarceration.'[18]

Law reform is one way of getting around this institutionalised racism, but attempts to date have been ineffective. For example:

- The Australian Law Reform Commission *Report into the Recognition of Aboriginal Customary Law*[19] was an expensive project which made recommendations into limited ways of recognising Aboriginal customary law. The final report was delivered in 1986. Not one of the recommendations has ever been implemented.

---

15 HREOC, 1999, p 84.
16 HREOC, 1999, p 92.
17 HREOC, 1999, p 92.
18 CERD/C/56/Misc42/para 16.
19 Australian Law Reform Commission, 1986, *Report into the Recognition of Aboriginal Customary Law*, Australian Government Publishing Service.

- The RCIADIC also made recommendations for improving the position of Aboriginal people within the criminal justice system. Since the Commission handed down its recommendations, the number of Aboriginal people in custody has increased and Aboriginal people in custody are dying at the same rate as the period that the Commission investigated (January 1980-May 1989).[20]

Not only are recommendations from major inquiries rarely implemented – or if they are, only half-heartedly – they seldom get to the root of the problems that cause the conflict between Aboriginal people and the criminal justice system. Changes within the criminal justice system do not change the poor socio-economic status of Aboriginal people. They do not change entrenched racist attitudes that parts of non-Aboriginal Australia have towards Indigenous people. They do not address the differences between the cultural values of Aboriginal society and those of the non-Aboriginal community. In addition, Indigenous people are such a small percentage of the population that they are often politically powerless to implement political change.

Yet, there are many individuals within the police force who are seeking to introduce initiatives which counter the dominant image of police attitudes towards Indigenous people. For example, the Saulwick and Muller research undertaken for the Council for Aboriginal Reconciliation found some of their focus group of police to be supportive of the reconciliation process. They identified that the respondents had sought to introduce partnerships and initiatives (such as Aboriginal liaison officers) with the Indigenous community despite the antagonistic attitudes within the non-Indigenous community in general. The study found that:

> [t]he police live on the ground. Some of the police to whom we spoke knew a lot about the Aboriginal people in their area. For example, they could talk about the tribal groups in their area and about tribal rivalries. They knew and listened to the elders. The elders, in turn, listened to them. Over time they were beginning to build real mutual respect. This in turn was leading to other examples of cooperation, such as where local Aboriginal auxiliary police were working to good effect in their own communities.[21]

---

20 Aboriginal and Torres Strait Islander Commission, 1995, *Annual Report 1994–1995*, Australian Government Publishing Service, p 129; J Behrendt and L Behrendt, 'Aboriginal Deaths in Custody Since the Royal Commission', 2(59) *Aboriginal Law Bulletin* 4 (December 1992).

21 M Grattan (ed), 2000, *Reconciliation*, Black Ink, p 42.

This shows that although there actually are sentiments within the police force that are supportive of reconciliation, this has not been enough to counter the impact of the legislation.

The most successful way that Indigenous communities are seeking to counter the disproportionate impact of the criminal justice system on their communities is through grass-roots initiatives that will provide greater community control over minor offences and juvenile delinquency. These community-based initiatives seek to rescue Indigenous people from the machinery of the state. These programs include the provision of 'dry areas' where intoxicated people can sober up and the imposition of punishments by community elders for juvenile crimes such as vandalism.

These alternatives indicate that the answer to the disparate impact of legislation such as mandatory sentencing lies not in harsher laws for minor crimes but alternative methods of punishment and atonement.

The last bastion: The Australian Constitution

The *'Stolen Generations* case' of *Kruger v Commonwealth*[22] was the first opportunity for the High Court to consider the legal infringements and remedies resulting from the policy of the forcible removal of Indigenous children.

The court was asked to consider questions relating to the validity of the *Aboriginals Ordinance* 1918 (NT). The plaintiffs, five people who had been taken from their families under the Ordinance and one parent who had lost a child under the same provision, sought a declaration that the Ordinance was invalid.

The case that the plaintiffs brought to court included arguments that the Ordinance contravened the protection of the freedom of religion in s 116 of the Constitution, infringed an implied freedom of movement, equality before the law and due process.

The case emphasised the fact that rights protection is primarily the responsibility of the legislature and highlights the inability of the Constitution to provide protection for Indigenous rights (and rights generally) and that this inhibits the High Court's ability to protect them. Indigenous people have had disappointing results when seeking redress for rights violations from the High Court and have been directed towards negotiation with the legislature.

---

22   *Kruger v Commonwealth* (1997) 190 CLR 1.

The *Stolen Generations* case drew attention to the undecided nature of the race power (s 51(xxvi) of the Constitution). Justice Gaudron gave weight to the argument that the race power only authorises laws for the benefit of the people of a race for whom it was necessary to make special laws.[23] On the other hand, Justices Gummow and Hayne observed that the race power had permitted detrimental as well as beneficial legislation.[24]

The argument that the federal government could only use the races power for the benefit of Indigenous people was again raised by the plaintiff in *Kartinyeri v Commonwealth* (the *Hindmarsh Island Bridge* case).[25] In that case, dealing with a dispute over a development site that the plaintiff had claimed was sacred to her, the government sought to settle the matter by passing legislation, the *Hindmarsh Island Bridge Act* 1997 (Cth). That Act was designed to repeal the application of heritage protection laws to the plaintiff (an example of the easy ability of Parliament to override legislated rights).

The plaintiff argued, *inter alia*, that when Australians voted in the 1967 Referendum to extend the Constitution's federal race power to include the power to make laws concerning Indigenous people, it was with the understanding that the power would only be used beneficially.

The court did not directly answer this issue, finding that the *Hindmarsh Island Bridge Act* 1997 merely repealed legislation. The majority held that the power to make laws also contains the power to repeal or amend them.

The symbolism of the case is important. This decision was seen as a victory by the Howard Government who saw constitutional challenges to amending legislation that extinguished native title rights as much harder to mount in light of their questionable constitutional protection. The question of the race power was not definitively answered, which leaves a serious issue undecided.

Consider the following exchange that took place during the arguments in front of the High Court between the Commonwealth Solicitor-General and Justice Kirby.[26]

---

23 At 362.
24 Gummow and Hayne JJ, at 379.
25 *Kartinyeri v Commonwealth* (1998) 195 CLR 337.
26 Reproduced in T Blackshield an G Williams, 2002, *Australian Constitutional Law and Theory: Commentary and Materials*, 3rd edn, The Federation Press, p 194.

Justice Kirby: Is the Commonwealth's submission that it is entirely and exclusively for the parliament to determine the matter upon which special laws are deemed necessary or ... there is a justiciable question for the court? I mean, it seems unthinkable that a law such as Nazi race laws could be enacted under the race power and that this court could do nothing about it.

Mr Gavan Griffith QC: Your Honour, if there was a reason why they could do something about it, a Nazi Law, it would, be for a reason external to the races power ...

In other words, the Commonwealth argued that it was constitutionally possible to use the race power to implement Nazi-style laws against Aboriginal people.

Many people were shocked to find that Australia's Constitution may offer no protection against racial discrimination but one need only look at the intention of the drafters to see why it could be argued as being the proper interpretation of the provision with so much confidence. In fact, a non-discrimination clause had been proposed in the Constitution when the instrument was being drafted.[27]

The following was proposed as s 110 of the Constitution.

> The citizens of each state, and all other persons owing allegiance to the Queen and residing in any territory of the Commonwealth, shall be citizens of the Commonwealth, and shall be entitled to all privileges and immunities of citizens of the Commonwealth in the several states; and a state shall not make or enforce any law abridging any privilege or immunity of citizens of the Commonwealth, nor shall a state deprive any person of life, liberty, or property without due process of law, or deny to any person within its jurisdiction the equal protection of its laws.

This clause was rejected for two reasons.

- It was believed that entrenched rights provisions were unnecessary and that the legislature was the proper arm of government to deal with the issue of rights.
- It was considered desirable to ensure that the Australian States would have the power to continue to enact laws that discriminated against people on the basis of their race.[28] It was considered

---

27 G Williams, 1999, *Human Rights under the Australian Constitution*, Oxford University Press, p 37.
28 Williams, 1999, pp 37-38.

desirable to regulate the movement of the Aboriginal and Chinese Australian populations. It was consistent with ideologies that embraced the notion of a 'White Australia' policy.

It should also be remembered that the 'doomed race' theory and social Darwinism were pervasive ideologies at the time the Constitution was drafted. If one is aware of these attitudes held by the drafters of the Constitution, then it comes as no surprise that the Constitution is a document that offers no protection against racial discrimination today. It was never intended to do so and the 1967 Referendum in no way addressed or challenged those fundamental principles that remain entrenched in the document.

Different conceptions of property

On Wednesday, 22 January 1997, the front page of the *Sydney Morning Herald* had news of a tragic fire in Melbourne. The photographs showed flames licking a house, charred bicycles and men fighting to save property. The newspapers were able to play an angle that evoked sympathy from Australians. The loss of property was emphasised in its human elements. On the left of the news of the fire was another news item. It was headed 'Aborigines set strong demands for *Wik* talks'. At that time, the *'Wik* talks' were the latest battleground in the fight by Aboriginal people for the recognition of their property rights by the laws, institutions and consciousness of the Australian people.

The media coverage of the *Wik* case was politically-loaded. The *Sydney Morning Herald* ran the headline that the *Wik* decision was 'A Decision for Chaos'. It printed a photograph of a farmer, a Mr Fraser, looking forlornly down at his land under the headline 'Family's land dream turns into nightmare'. Although he claimed to be a strong supporter of 'the Aborigines' and said he believes in reconciliation, he was 'confused' by the decision. Mr Fraser's reaction was one of bewilderment.

> I can't believe these judges made that decision. It's not a decision. I can't see that we have made very much progress. We are obviously going through another period of indecision and I am not sure how much of that sort of punishment people can take.[29]

---

29 J Woodford, 1996, 'Family's land dream turns into nightmare', *Sydney Morning Herald*, 24 December, p 1.

What the coverage of the paper showed was three *contemporary* perceptions in the public consciousness.

- That the loss of property — houses, bicycles, cars — was seen as a tragedy when (white) people lost their homes, but when Aboriginal people lose a property right, it does not have a human aspect to it.
- Aboriginal people, in getting recognition of a property right, are seen as gaining something (making 'strong demands') rather than having recognised something that already exists and should be protected.
- Aboriginal property interests are seen as threatening the interests of white property owners. The two cannot co-exist. Recognition of Aboriginal rights leads to 'uncertainty' and 'indecision'.

These three perceptions — that there is no human aspect to Aboriginal property rights, that Aborigines and Torres Strait Islanders are getting something for nothing and that white property interests are more valuable than black ones — are not just played out in the headlines of that Sydney newspaper. Their influence can be found pervasively throughout the history of colonised Australia, starting from the day that the British declared Australia was theirs on the basis of a legal fiction — that the land was *terra nullius*: vacant.

These contemporary perceptions assist in the rewriting and revising of Australia's historical treatment of Indigenous peoples, allowing a sanitised, temporal re-imagination. The way in which Australians perceive Aboriginal land rights reveals much about their perception of their own history and their sense of nationalism. These perceptions underlie every aspect of Australian life and are found most strikingly in the way that Australian law has operated separately for Aboriginal and non-Aboriginal peoples. For most Australians, the right to own property and to have property interests protected is a central and essential part of their legal system. For Aborigines, Australian law has operated to deny property rights, then acknowledge them sparingly only to extinguish them again.

Understanding the way in which Australian property law distinguishes between Aboriginal property interests and those of other Australians involves understanding what land means to Indigenous Australians, how Indigenous property rights were extinguished as part of the conquering of Australia by the non-Aborigines and investigating how these historical perspectives have permeated contemporary Australian institutions.

Indigenous relationships to land

> We bond with the universe and the land and everything that exists on the land. Everyone is bonded to everything.
>
> Ownership for the white people is something on a piece of paper. We have a different system. You can no more sell our land than sell the sky.
>
> Our affinity with the land is like the bonding between a parent and a child. You have responsibilities and obligations to look after and care for a child. You can speak for a child. But you don't own a child.

That is the way that my father, Paul Behrendt, explained my place in the world and my cultural relationship to land. The relationship of Indigenous people to traditional land is best understood in its multifaceted nature. With subtle regional differences, all Indigenous groups have a religion which derives its beliefs and values from the period of creation, referred to now as the Dreaming or the Dreamtime.[30] During this period, the world was created by super beings who created the land, humans and animals. These spirits then returned to the rocks and ground and water and sky and still live in the landscape. With this knowledge, the landscape becomes rich with religious symbolism as spirits of ancestors are believed to dwell in rivers, stones and mountains.

Djon Mundine describes the Dreamtime in the following way: 'the nebulous term Dreamtime can be best described as the reality of the spirit world. It exists at the beginning of time, in the present, and continues into the future.'[31]

Heather Goodall identifies the 'sense of profound authority' and 'sacredness' of Dreamtime knowledge.

> It is composed of a body of oral tradition held in memory and taught in performance as the words and music of songs, as painting and dance. All of these performed works are celebrations of and communications with existing Dreamings about which they speak. Dreaming events are set in a period long past, far beyond everyday

---

30 H Goodall, 1996, *Invasion to Embassy: Land in Aboriginal Politics in New South Wales, 1770–1972*, Allen & Unwin.

31 D Mundine, 1999, 'The Land is Full of Signs: Central North East Arnhem Land Art' in H Morphy and MS Boles (eds), *Art of the Land*, University of Virginia Press, p 85.

experiences of time, but this 'dreaming time' also continues, separate from every day and parallel to it.[32]

Land has a strong spiritual and religious meaning associated with the law stories of the Dreamtime. Indigenous people understand that the land gives life. Bequeathed by Elders, religious stories and ceremonies breathed life into the land and people develop strong affiliations and intimate ties to their country. This relationship is one of custodianship or guardianship, embodying rights and responsibilities including ensuring that the resources of a certain area are maintained. The landscape is richly symbolic and ancestral land becomes personal as one is obliged to look after it and ensure its natural balance. Land belonging to others has no meaning to someone who was a stranger to it, since specific tracts of land are special to the group who understand the lore and history of that country.

There is also a newer historical memory imprinted onto land as a result of the experiences of colonialism, creating new symbolism on the landscape.[33] People remember where camps were destroyed, people were massacred and children taken away. Many Indigenous people have been involuntarily moved off their traditional lands, are unable to return and are denied access to their traditional country. Yet the land, just like the sea, remains important to Indigenous people even if the nature of that relationship has changed.

Galarrwuy Yunupingu, the former Chair of the Northern Land Council, has spoken of the central role land continues to play in Indigenous life.

> Recognition of land rights is the key to Aboriginal self determination. It is the basis for our development of a secure social, cultural and economic base. It gives us the basis for claiming compensation and achieving proper health, education, legal and child care services. The constitution must restore our rights to land under

---

32 Goodall, 1996, p 3.
33 'There were similar echoes of traditional meanings for land in the way which people identified themselves with land, and orientated their relationships with each other in terms of that association. There were further meanings, however, which rose from the memories of the intense experiences of violence and repressive colonisation, the memories of massacre and dispossessions, both long past and very recent. Then there were the many 'everyday' memories, the experiences of lifetimes passed on the one site, while others were memories of the warmth as well as the tensions of community life': Goodall, 1996, pp 348-49.

secure title, guarantee our access to lands and sites of Aboriginal significance on land which cannot be restored to us, give us full control of our own lands and compensate us for our lands which have been alienated.[34]

Non-Indigenous people may think that dispossessed Indigenous people living within a city have lost their connections to their traditional land. The needs of urban Indigenous communities may also seem no different to the needs of other Australians, but there is a unique historical context created by the experience of dispossession by force and under the laws of Australia. The RCIADIC *National Report* noted this, observing that Indigenous people living in urban communities draw a contrast between Indigenous and non-Indigenous ways, especially between Indigenous and non- Indigenous values. The Report notes:

> their [the Aborigines] social relations remain focused on the facts of kinship and ties of family. Kin associations permeate most aspects of their life and they feel a great passion about their ties to land and their concern over diminishing access to lands, rivers and coast for hunting and fishing ... Although they cannot now identify particular areas of land as being owned in traditional law by particular ancestors, they have a lively awareness that their forefathers had all those traditional relationships with the land ...[35]

Urbanised and dispossessed Indigenous communities stress that they need land as an economic base. The acquisition of land by an Indigenous community is seen as a step towards being independent and therefore not having to be answerable to the government. Housing in urban communities is also seen as a land rights issue. Communities believe that land acquisition will allow for long-term planning and development that will eventually raise the status of Indigenous people.

Although Indigenous groups throughout Australia are culturally diverse, land was always, and continues to be, the source of social, spiritual and legal arrangements. This system — based on duty, reciprocity and custodianship — conflicted with the British legal notions of private possession.

---

34 G Yunupingu, 1987, 'What the Aboriginal People Want', *The Age*, 26 August; reprinted in B Attwood and A Markus (eds), 1999, *The Struggle for Aboriginal Rights: A Documentary History*, Allen & Unwin, p 314.

35 RCIADIC, 1991, vol 2, para 19.1.4.

Dispossession: The doctrine of Terra Nullius

Australia was claimed by the British on the basis that it was *terra nullius:* vacant and/or without a sovereign.[36] This claim ignored the international standards of the time, failed to recognise the sovereignty of Indigenous Australians and overlooked customary laws, including property laws. The British, through the use of the doctrine of *terra nullius*, created a myth that the land was 'settled' by them. Institutionalised in the legal system, this legal fiction was more convenient and better suited to the aims of a colony that sought to expand its frontiers and establish a lucrative pastoral industry. It was supported by Eurocentric notions of property use, influenced by the Lockean concept of mixing labour with the soil. Since land use was so radically different between the two cultures, Europeans dismissed Indigenous use of and relations to the land as wasteful, trivial and primitive. The lack of fences, public buildings and hard agricultural power of labour encouraged interpretations that the Aborigines were nomadic with no significant attachment to their land.

Despite claims that there were no Indigenous property rights, the British saw themselves from the earliest days of the colony as being in competition with Indigenous people for land. Australia's first farmers often used land without government sanction, believed they were the key to the (economic) future of the colony and sought long-term tenure over leases. Aboriginal people had an incongruous relationship to the pastoralists. Indigenous rights to land conflicted with the colonial agenda, yet farmers needed Aboriginal and Torres Strait Islander people to support their system by providing cheap or slave labour. Aboriginal reserves were supported by pastoralists who wanted this pool of labour confined and supervised nearby.[37] Especially during the gold rush, Australia's pastoral industry could not have carried on without the labour of Indigenous people. The faithfulness of Aboriginal people to runs or farms on their traditional land made them loyal workers. It was here that dual occupancy emerged as an ideal arrangement, with farmers allowing Indigenous people to remain on pastoral leases in return for a pool of inexpensive labour.[38]

---

36 Goodall, 1996, p 61.
37 Goodall, 1996, p 61.
38 Ibid.

Governments and churches were supposed to represent and protect Indigenous interests but their aims, concerned with the assimilation and Christianising of Indigenous peoples, conflicted with those of Aboriginal and Torres Strait Islander communities (to reclaim land and maintain cultural practices). The statutory body designed to protect Indigenous interests in NSW, the Aborigines Protection Board, failed to act in the best interests of the Aboriginal people. It sold off Aboriginal land to fund its policy of removing children and leased Aboriginal land for its own revenues, sometimes even interrupting the successful leases of Aboriginal farmers to lease lands to white farmers. Even today, land becomes alienated from Aboriginals for the use of pastoral leases, urban development and mining opportunities, diminishing the rights of Indigenous people to stay on traditional lands.

The loss of land was crippling to Indigenous communities. Only ancestral land was of value to Indigenous people; attachment was non-transferable. Not only were Indigenous communities less capable of surviving in unfamiliar territory but religious life was also seriously impaired or even lost. Traditional aspects of Aboriginal culture were also threatened when groups were massacred, had their children taken away or were removed from ancestral lands as oral traditions could not be passed down to younger generations. Throughout this period, the imposed British legal system did not recognise or protect Indigenous rights to traditional land, becoming complicit in the dispossession of Indigenous people.

The Land Rights Acts: Benevolence not recognition

Legislative instruments were passed to establish schemes to allow Indigenous people to claim land in certain circumstances.[39] The *Aboriginal Land Rights (Northern Territory) Act* 1976 (Cth) was an initiative of the Whitlam Government, amended and diluted but at least passed under the subsequent Fraser Government. It only applied to the Northern Territory so States had to follow with similar legislation. States and Territories did pass legislation but those land

---

39 Legislation was passed in South Australia to allow the Pitjantjantjara special control over their traditional land, *Pitjantjantjara Land Rights Act* 1981 (SA). This legislation was exceptional in that it was far more generous than subsequent legislation but was also linked especially to traditional lands — which land rights legislations never did.

grants were seen as gifts and as recompense for land already lost, not recognition of rights to land that still existed. 'Land rights' were often seen as a special privilege and greatly resented by some Australians who viewed it as gaining something for nothing.

For example, the Western Australian Chamber of Mines ran a virulent campaign against land rights legislation in that State in 1984, ensuring the defeat of the legislation. Its anti-land rights campaign focused on creating fear within the general population by implying — erroneously — that people's homes would be at risk. 'Your right of ownership could be under threat', their advertisement thundered. A television commercial, playing on this fear, showed black hands building a brick wall across a map of Western Australia with an accompanying sign: 'Keep out — this land is part of Western Australia under Aboriginal land claim'.[40] If Western Australia thought Indigenous land claims would impede economic development in their state as the Western Australian Chamber of Mines campaign threatened, they only needed to look at the experience in the Northern Territory where 80 per cent of mining revenue comes from land owned by Aboriginal communities.[41] By 1991, the Northern Territory Land Councils claimed that they had entered into agreements for exploration on over 35,000 square kilometers of Indigenous land.[42]

For those jurisdictions that did implement land claims, each legislative regime was different, with some schemes focused on land claims and others on financial compensation. None allowed for the claim of privately-owned land.

In the Northern Territory, the focus was on land claims with traditional owners being able to claim unalienated Crown land.[43] The Queensland legislation also focused on traditional association and on economic and cultural needs.[44] The NSW scheme, under the *Aboriginal Land Rights Act* 1983 (NSW) allowed for 7.5 per cent of revenue from State land tax for 15 years to be collected for Aboriginal use. Half was to be invested and the other half was to be used for making land claims and for purchasing land.

---

40 C Cunneen and T Libesman, 1995, *Indigenous People and the Law in Australia*, Butterworths, p 139.
41 Cunneen and Libesman, 1995, p 141.
42 Cunneen and Libesman, 1995, p 142.
43 *Aboriginal Land Rights (Northern Territory) Act* 1976 (Cth).
44 *Aboriginal Land Act* 1991 (Qld) and *Torres Strait Islander Land Act* 1991 (Qld).

Land has been gained back by Indigenous peoples under these legislative schemes and despite the racist fear-mongering of the mining interests and the resentment of some sectors of the Australian community, there are others who have supported the schemes as appropriate remedial measures to counter past injustices leading to Indigenous dispossession.

However, there are some ideological underpinnings to the land rights legislation that deserve notice. The NSW Act was interpreted by the judiciary as 'beneficial and remedial' legislation which should be given the 'most beneficial operation compatible with its language'.[45] The Long Title of that Act states:

> An Act to ... make provisions with respect to the land rights of Aborigines, including provisions for or with respect to the constitution of Aboriginal Land Councils, the vesting of land in those Councils, the vesting of land in those Councils, the acquisition of land by or for those Councils and the allocations of funds to and by those Councils; to amend certain other Acts; and to make provisions for certain other purposes.

This may seem to imply that this was a recognition of 'land rights' but traditional interests in land were assumed to have been erased. The Preamble of that Act bears this out:

> *Whereas:*
> (1) Land in the State of New South Wales was traditionally owned and occupied by Aborigines;
> (2) Land is of spiritual, social, cultural and economic importance to Aborigines;
> (3) It is fitting to acknowledge the importance which land has for Aborigines and the need of Aborigines for land;
> (4) It is accepted that as a result of past Government decisions the amount of land set aside for Aborigines had been progressively reduced without compensation ...

These sentiments recognise pre-existing rights and continuing attachment without recognising *existing* property rights. The final point in the Preamble also makes clear that this is a provision to compensate for past government policies that have not been benevolent enough to Indigenous people but will be more benevolent now.

---

45 *Minister for Natural Resources v New South Wales Aboriginal Land Council* (1987) 9 NSWLR 154 at 157 per Kirby P.

Under the Act, Indigenous people could claim certain vacant Crown land that met the criteria although there was nothing in the Act that linked claims to land with traditional attachments. Nor, importantly, was there anything in the Act that recognised prior ownership or property interests of Indigenous peoples.

Despite this benevolence, the claims process under the NSW Act was complicated, political and, in practice, difficult. In order to claim land under the Act, the Aboriginal community, through a Local Land Council or the NSW Aboriginal Land Council, needed to meet the criteria set out in s 36. While the Act meant that Indigenous people could make a claim over any Crown land not needed for an essential public purpose or for residential development as set out in s 36, in practice, claims were hard to make since s 36(8) allowed the Crown Lands Minister to issue a certificate stating that the land was needed for future purposes. This certificate, which did not need to specify the particular essential public purpose, was 'final and conclusive', could not be 'called into question' and was not 'liable to appeal or review on any grounds whatever'.[46]

The benevolence of the Act also gains some perspective when it is realised that Indigenous people actually *lost* vast amounts of land when NSW eventually passed the *Aboriginal Land Rights Act* 1983 (NSW). It had been discovered that the Crown land had been vested in the Aboriginal Protection Board until 1969, not the Lands Department. This made all revocations of Crown land from Aboriginal reserves by the Lands Department (a total of 25,000 acres) invalid. To 'rectify' this mistake, the *Retrospective Validation of Revocations Act* 1983 (NSW) was passed. This Act validated the reserve land taken from Aboriginal people. Thus when the NSW State government passed the *Aboriginal Land Rights Act* 1983 (NSW), it was handing over 6000 acres — but removed hopes of regaining the 25,000 that had been lost through the illegal actions of the Lands Department.

Even if potentially benevolent and seen as recompense for lost land, these legislative schemes assumed that there was no Indigenous right to land independent of the statutory entitlement and often masked further acts of dispossession. It should also be remembered that these remedial and benevolent pieces of legislation fostered great antagonism within the non-Indigenous community, who resented

---

46 *Aboriginal Land Rights Act* 1983 (NSW), s 36(8).

what they saw as Aborigines 'getting something for nothing' and they feared a threat to their own title to land (even though land rights legislation ensured that this would not happen). These fears and phobias resurfaced in the debates around the recognition of native title.

The Mabo decision:
Recognition of an existing property right

In 1992, the *Mabo* case[47] defined native title as a right that exists when an Indigenous community can show that there is a continuing association with the land and that no explicit act of the government, federal or State, has extinguished that title. Radical title was vested in the Crown of the 'discovering' nation — or the subsequent independent, once-colonial government — but the Indigenous people retained the right of occupancy although they could dispose of their land to the Crown. It is important to emphasise that the court *recognised* rather than created native title, that is, native title had existed, unacknowledged, all along.

The High Court held that native title exists in the manner in which it is defined by the Aboriginal laws and customs. It is those practices that will determine the parameters of the native title. Native title is held communally. It can be extinguished by legislation that has a clear and plain intent to do so. The majority of the court found that compensation was not payable under common law for extinguishment. In fact, the pronouncement in the *Mabo* case meant that for many Indigenous people, the Australian law had confirmed that their traditional property interests had been extinguished long ago. It was estimated that the result in the *Mabo* case would assist only 5 per cent of the Indigenous population.[48]

There are several factors that explain the High Court's decision to overturn the doctrine of *terra nullius* when it did.

- There was an evolving political climate in 1992 where there was a better understanding of the experiences of Indigenous people in Australia and a greater respect for the culture of Indigenous people by the dominant Australian culture.

---

47 *Mabo v Queensland (No 2)* (1992) 175 CLR 1.
48 Aboriginal and Torres Strait Islander Social Justice Commission, 1993, *First Report 1993*, Australian Government Publishing Service, p 16.

- The court could frame the finding so that it was, in effect, a narrow concession. Given the amount of removal of Indigenous people from traditional land as a government policy since the time of invasion up until recent times, there are very few Indigenous groups that would fulfill the criteria of native title, especially the need to show a continuing attachment to land.
- The court ignored many serious questions that the recognition of native title raised, leaving those to be decided by future litigation. These included:
  - whether pastoral leases and mining leases extinguish native title (which was not raised as an issue); and
  - whether the principles of native title in land extend to fishing rights (which was specifically excluded from the question posed to the court by the applicant).
- Indigenous people have become better organised and more adept at using the legal system now that most communities have representation through Aboriginal Land Councils and other community-based organisations.

Native title, although often conceptualised as an 'Indigenous right', is also a property right with parallels to many other property rights. In fact, in many ways, native title is no different to already recognised, and uncontroversial, property rights such as easements. Its communal nature is also analogous to other property holdings such as property held by corporations. The co-existence of the interests is like many competing interests over a piece of property: mortgagors/mortgagees, landlords/tenants. Given the fact that native title shares characteristics with other property rights and the fairly minimal parameters given to the interest in the *Mabo case*, the divisive, passionate controversy surrounding its recognition needs to be explored.

Modern Australia is a country that is built on the land of its Indigenous people, land that was stolen in sometimes vicious, illegal and deceitful actions, land that created wealth through pastoral and mining industries.

It is no surprise that farmers and miners have been the most vehement opponents to the decision in the *Mabo* case. Both groups actively lobbied through often blatantly false propaganda to have the decision overturned by the legislature and took no pains to hide the political nature of their resistance to the recognition of native title interests.

THE MYTH OF LAW'S NEUTRALITY

Advocates for mining and pastoral interests resorted to scare tactics, modelled on the anti-land rights legislation rhetoric. Australians were led to believe that Aboriginal statehood was the real goal and that the High Court's decision made freehold land vulnerable to claims.

Lobbyists and mining companies fed this ignorance by warning that the decision in the *Mabo* case could lead to the confiscation of private property (freehold), an underhanded lie easily dismissed by a cursory reading of the law. Self-interested groups have characterised the recognition of native title as the giving to Indigenous people an interest in land for free, thus feeding the racist prejudices of sections of the Australian population, ignorant of the barbarities of their own history and conveniently failing to recall the enormous theft of Indigenous land.

For example, Hugh Morgan, CEO of Western Mining Corporation, stated:

> As far the campaigners are concerned, they have made it crystal clear that their endeavours, extending over two generations, will only be concluded when a separate, sovereign Aboriginal state is carved out of Australia. We can reasonably predict that this Aboriginal state will have all the trappings of sovereignty, but will rely almost entirely on subvention from Australia and its continuing existence.

and

> If the Kimberleys becomes the focus for the politics of Aboriginal sovereignty the WA Government, and the people of Western Australia, will be faced eventually either with acquiescence in the loss of a major part of their territory of Western Australia, or secession from the Commonwealth of Australia. That will not be an easy decision to make.[49]

None of these assertions are true nor have these predictions of separatism come to pass. Resistance to the *Mabo* decision also derives from a confusion of the issues of sovereignty and property. Recognising the existence of Indigenous communities at the time of 'discovery' may have implications for the sovereignty of Indigenous people but this issue was not determined in the *Mabo* case. In the *Mabo*

---

49   H Morgan, 1992, 'The Dangers of Aboriginal Sovereignty', *News Weekly*, 29 August, p 13.

case, as in earlier cases that raised the issue of Aboriginal sovereignty, the High Court stated that the issue was not one that could be considered by the domestic courts of Australia.

The Keating Government sought to clarify interests, secure title, regulate procedures and set up the National Native Title Tribunal to hear claims under the *Native Title Act* 1993 (Cth). The *Native Title Act* provided for, *inter alia*:

- the validation of all existing land grants, with native title to be extinguished in all but mining leases (an act that extinguished native title);
- States to validate existing land titles without suspending the *Racial Discrimination Act* 1975 (Cth), using a provision designed to ensure Aborigines receive rights to negotiate; and
- lessees' rights to have primacy over those of native title holders. Aborigines were be able to negotiate over land use but could not veto it.

On 30 June 1994, before the *Native Title Act* became law, the Wik and Thayorre peoples made a native title claim on the Cape York Peninsula in Queensland. The High Court attempted to clarify one of the grey areas created by the *Mabo* case: the issue of whether pastoral leases and mining leases extinguished native title. The High Court said that native title can only be extinguished by a written law or an Act of the government that shows a clear and plain intention to extinguish. The Queensland lease in the case before the court did not show such an intention. The High Court held by a majority that pastoral leases did not give exclusive possession to the pastoralists and that the grant of a pastoral lease does not extinguish native title interests. Native title can co-exist with a pastoral lease but if the interests of the land holders conflicted, the native title interests would be subordinate; that is, the native title rights need to be consistent with the rights in the pastoral lease to co-exist – they need to be exercisable without interfering with the rights and interests provided by the pastoral lease. This co-existence of native title interests and leasehold interests reflects arrangements informally created by pastoralists who allowed Indigenous people access to traditional sites and whose properties had supported communities of Indigenous people as a pool of cheap labour.

The court held that a native title holder cannot exclude the holder of a pastoral lease from the area covered by the pastoral lease or restrict pastoralists from using the lease area for pastoral purposes. Nor can a native title holder interfere with:

- the pastoralist's ability to use land and water on their leasehold;
- the pastoralist's privacy; or
- the pastoralist's right to build fences or make other improvements to the land.

Whenever there is a conflict between the use under the lease by the pastoralist and the Indigenous people's native title interest, the interest of the farmer will always triumph. Pastoralists do not even pay for the infringement or extinguishment of native title interests. Any compensation is payable by the government.

The legal interests of farmers remain unchanged; there was no impact on the value of the pastoral lease. Financial institutions base their loans on the property's capacity to carry stock (its ability to generate income), the equipment owned by the pastoralists and improvements to the land. These matters were unaffected by the *Wik* decision. It was only the pastoralists' *perception* of their property rights that changed. As with the result in the *Mabo* case, the decision in the *Wik* case ignited public hysteria that was further fuelled by the deceitful misrepresentations of industry and government. Government propaganda scared farmers by telling them that Aborigines could claim their land.

Continued dispossession:
The Native Title Amendment Act

The Howard Government's response to the *Wik* case was laid out in its proposal to implement a '10 Point Plan'. This plan suggested the extinguishment of native title interests by converting the leasehold interest into a freehold interests — a windfall to the farmers since they would gain freehold title of land they currently held as leasehold (ie, they would get something for nothing). The cost of conversion and any compensation that would become payable due to an extinguishment of native title was to be covered by the public purse. Indigenous peoples would lose, even if compensation was payable. If the native title interest was the right to enter the land and perform a ceremony, the monetary amount payable for the extinguishment of that right would fail to compensate for the substance of the right being lost. The remuneration did not account for cultural and religious practices being lost. Aboriginal people preferred to keep their property interest.

During the development of the 10 Point Plan and its justification for extinguishment of native title interests, the Federal Government sought to create the image that pastoral leaseholders are small family-run farms. The reality is that the industry is dominated by big individual and corporate farmers. Cheryl Kernot, the then leader of the Australian Democrat Party, noted that 'a search of register of members of Federal Parliament reveals that no fewer than 20 members and nine senators, representing the Liberal, National, One Nation and Labor parties, have interests in farming, grazing or pastoral activities.'[50] Along with those members of Parliament are some of Australia's richest individuals; foreign-controlled corporations also have rural landholdings of more than 7 million hectares.[51]

With this windfall at stake, it was little wonder that the mining and pastoral industries pushed the Liberal Government to take an inflexible line with the proposed Bill. Senator Herron, the Minister for Aboriginal Affairs, stated his commitment clearly.

> The backbone of this country, I'm proud to say, are the pastoralists. I have no doubt the wisdom they will bring to the judgment they deliver, in the development of policy, will be to the betterment of this country as a whole ... I'm quite proud of the fact there are so many pastoralists on our side, in both the Liberal Party and the National Party ...[52]

---

50 A Ramsey, 1997, 'Ramsey's View: Conflict of interest? So what?', *Sydney Morning Herald*, 10 May. The Liberal Party funds itself on shares held in mining companies, including CSR Ltd (formerly Colonial Sugar Refining Co Ltd) and Conzinc Riotinto of Australia Ltd (CRA): A Davies, 1997, 'Bluebloods fund Libs with blue-chip shares', *Sydney Morning Herald*, 23 December. The protection of Indigenous property rights are further jeopardised by the apparent conflict of interest when a Government Minister has a financial interest in mining companies. For instance, Federal Resources Minister Warwick Parer was found to have (undisclosed) interests in a mine worth $2 million. Prime Minister Howard supported Parer's claim that there was no conflict of interest, stating that the interest had been transferred to Parer's wife: M Seccombe and G Roberts, 1998, 'Mining His Own Business', *Sydney Morning Herald*, 21 March; L Tingle, 1998, 'Parer linked to new mine group', *Sydney Morning Herald*, 24 March; R Skelton and G Roberts, 1998, 'Parer crisis escalates as Japan meeting revealed', *Sydney Morning Herald*, 20 March.

51 D Jopson and I Verrender, 1997, 'Richest of Rich are Wik Winners', *Sydney Morning Herald*, 10 May.

52 Jopson and Verrender, 1997.

THE MYTH OF LAW'S NEUTRALITY

The Native Title Amendment Bill which contained the 10 Point Plan reflected the extent to which Indigenous stakeholders had been dismissed by the Prime Minister and his supporters. The Bill was revised in the Upper House to allow Aboriginal people the right to negotiate. The Howard Government rejected the amended Bill and tried again three months later to get the Senate to pass it in its original form. Howard again refused to compromise on the issues and rejected the amendments made by the Senate. The Government's uncompromising line and its rhetoric regarding business uncertainty ignored the fact that there have been successfully negotiated agreements between Indigenous communities with native title or other interests and mining or pastoral companies.[53]

The Prime Minister continued to push an approach informed by the ideologies of white Australian nationalism and the doctrine of *terra nullius*. This link to the ideologies of the past is evident in the words of Hugh Morgan:

> When we look back, however, over the period since Sir Robert Menzies retired, just over 25 years ago, and observe how, bit by bit, the language of cultural despair has been adopted by Ministers of the Crown; how the politics of guilt have become the bi-partisan stock in trade of Government and Opposition; how vast tracts of land have been allocated to Aborigines, on the basis of race and descent, under unique terms (terms which effectively take land out of the Australian economy); it is impossible to avoid the conclusion that very powerful forces are at work in our hearts and minds. We seem to have lost our self-respect, and we have certainly lost our admiration for the pioneers who came here from Europe over a century ago and developed this land.[54]

Morgan plays a clever semantic trick here. By claiming that land claimed by Aboriginal Australians have been 'allocated' on the 'basis of race and descent', he is decontextualising the principle behind the land rights movement and principles in *Wik* (that Aboriginal people had legitimate property interests in land that were illegally ignored). Without this context, Morgan portrays the rights of Indigenous peoples as being 'something for nothing', made even more abhorrent by the fact that it is a windfall based on race (ironically, the same

---

53 J Woodford, 1997, 'Native Title's $1bn victory', *Sydney Morning Herald*, 28 March. See also I Manning, 1997, *Native Title, Mining, and Mineral Exploration*, National Institute of Economic Industry and Research.

54 Morgan, 1992, p 13.

reason why the land was lost in the first place since Aboriginal property rights were not afforded the same legal recognition as non-Indigenous claims). Morgan seeks to block this objection by raising the alarm that talk of the historical context is only the 'politics of guilt'. It is in this rhetorical, semantic play that many Australians find comfort – a retelling of their history that romanticises the 'pioneers who came here from Europe'. It is this kind of storytelling that allows Morgan to create a myth of settlement and to create a psychological *terra nullius*.

The recognition of Aboriginal property rights (or lack thereof) has two ideological strands:

- the notion of national identity;
- competition for economic resources and profit.

The first leads to a denial of the presence of Indigenous people and a failure to recognise their pre-existing property rights. As 'other' to the national image, there is resentment and envy that Indigenous peoples might control rich resources. Similarly, economic motivations, not without racist undertones, perpetuate a sense of envy and resentment as Aborigines are perceived as 'getting something for nothing'. These ideologies combine to form a mixture of forces that perpetually deny the recognition of the property rights of Aboriginal people.

When the *Native Title Amendment Act* 1998 (Cth) was finally passed, after a deal made between the Coalition Government and (Independent) Senator Brian Harradine, it resulted in the following:

- a reduction in the say of native title holders about exploration in their traditional country (some schemes of consultation);
- the replacement of the right to negotiate on pastoral leases through States-based legislation;
- a full range of primary production activities allowed on current pastoral leases without negotiating with the co-existent native title holders.
- a reduction in the say of native title holders in a whole range of government activities on their traditional land.
- tougher conditions for native title holders presenting cases in claims hearings.

These rights further eroded native title interests, seeming to forget that Indigenous people in the *Native Title Act* debates had conceded rights in order to gain the ability to have control over land which had a native title interest. The right to negotiate was considered to be essential by Indigenous people at that time and was weakened by these amendments.

Indigenous people and their representative groups such as the Aboriginal and Torres Strait Islander Commission (ATSIC) were angered by the proposed legislation. Not only did it erode native title rights by further extinguishment but Indigenous people were not properly consulted about the proposed changes to legislation that would profoundly affect their rights. Olga Havnen, former Executive Officer of the National Indigenous Working Group, reflected on this exclusion.

> Although native title rights and interests — our rights and interests — were at the core of this debate, from the outset the Prime Minister barely paid lip service to any consultation with either the Working Group or ATSIC when formulating the 10-point plan and we were completely excluded from the negotiations which led to the final agreement between Harradine and Howard.[55]

Prime Minister John Howard was concerned to ensure that other sectors of the community were informed and consulted. His address to the Longreach Community Meeting in Queensland is revealing. He begins his speech by describing the rural idyll of the 'white man on the land'.

> [A]lthough I was born in Sydney and I lived all my life in the urban parts of Australia, I have always had an immense affection for the bush. I say that because in all of my political life no charge would offend me more, than the suggestion that what I've done and what I've believe in has not taken proper account of the concerns of the Australian bush.[56]

---

55 O Havnen, 2000, 'The Native Title Amendment Act', in L Strelein and K Muir (eds), *Native Title in Perspective: Selected Papers from the Native Title Research Unit 1998–2000*, Native Title Research Unit, Australian Institute of Aboriginal and Torres Strait Islander Studies, p 13.

56 J Howard, 2000a, 'Address to Participants at the Longreach Community Meeting to Discuss the Wik 10 Point Plan, Longreach, Queensland.' Transcript, reproduced in Parliamentary Joint Committee on Native Title and the Aboriginal and Torres Strait Islander Land Fund, *CERD and the Native Title Amendment Act 1998*, Parliament of the Commonwealth of Australia, p 276.

There is no such concern for Indigenous people who clearly do not fulfil this same sentimental, nationalistic ideology. He then proceeds to rank the rights of one over the rights of the other.

> [T]he plan the Federal Government has will deliver the security, and the guarantees to which the pastoralists of Australia are entitled ...[57]
>
> Because under the guarantees that will be contained in this legislation, the right to negotiate, that stupid property right that was given to native title claimants alone, unlike other title holders in Australia, that native title right will be completely abolished and removed for all time ...
>
> That if there are any compensation payments ordered to be made in relation to the compulsory acquisition or compulsory resumption of any established native title rights anywhere in Australia, that compensation will not be borne by the pastoralists of Australia, it will be borne by the general body of the Australian taxpayers ...[58]

An increase in the property interest of pastoralists, at the taxpayers expense, is not characterised as 'something for nothing'. The right of the native title holder to negotiate is dismissed as merely the tool of troublemakers, not a valid property interest that is rooted in a cultural, legal and historical relationship.

> We knew the right to negotiate was a licence for people to come from nowhere and make a claim on your property and then say until you pay me out, we're not going to allow you to do anything with your property. Well let me say I regard that as repugnant, and I regard that as un-Australian and unacceptable and that is going to be removed by the amendments that are already in the Federal Parliament. You won't have to put up with that anymore ...[59]

John Howard, in fact, characterises the exercise to protect a property right as 'un-Australian'.

Olga Havnen notes the irony of the *Native Title Amendment Act* being referred to as a 'special measure'.

> [I]t seems that other parties have had major windfall gains out of what was supposed to be a win for us, particularly out of the Wik case. In contrast, our rights have been significantly wound back or in other situations our native title has been extinguished outright. For

---

57 Howard, 2000a, p 276.
58 Howard, 2000a, p 277.
59 Howard, 2000a, p 278.

these reasons it would be impossible to characterise the NTAA as a 'special measure' ...[60]

Geoff Clark, the Chairman of Aboriginal and Torres Strait Islander Commission, also reflected on the outcome of the *Native Title Act* amendments.

> If Indigenous people are not involved, or if we are excluded from the process, the people who are making the decisions give what they consider us to be worthy of, which is not what Indigenous people consider to be our rights.[61]

Native title: Not like any other property rights

Many have argued that native title should have greater protection than other property right: since native title was *sui generis*, unique, it should be accorded special status; since it was derived from Indigenous law, it should not be simply categorised to fit neatly within the property frameworks of British-derived property laws. For example, Noel Pearson, adviser to, and former Chairman of, the Cape York Land Council, has said:

> The equating of Aboriginal titles with normal titles obscures the very nature of Aboriginal title. Aboriginal title arises out of the customs and laws of the Aboriginal titleholders; nothing in mainstream titles is comparable. The High Court in *Mabo* clearly stated that indigenous title is *sui generis* (of its own kind) and that it is misleading to attempt to define the title by resort to English property law concepts.[62]

Those who sought to draw attention to the unique legal, historical and cultural aspects of native title and to gain heightened protection for it must have been sobered by the fact that it failed to receive even the *same* recognition as other property interests. Property rights held by Indigenous Australians had no status under law and now have an uncertain legal status — uncertain because so many areas are left

---

60 Havnen, 2000, p 13.
61 G Clark, 2000a, 'Native Title and the Political Environment', in L Strelein and K Muir (eds), *Native Title in Perspective: Selected Papers from the Native Title Research Unit 1998–2000*, Native Title Research Unit, Australian Institute of Aboriginal and Torres Strait Islander Studies, p 1.
62 'Law Must Dig Deeper to Find Land Rights', *The Australian*, 8 June 1993.

unclear in the *Mabo* case and uncertain because the legislature has sought to limit the scope of the legal decision and to extinguish certain native title rights. Yet property rights are central to the English legal system and, in other contexts, are protected tenaciously.

Under Australian law, property has been deemed to:

> extend to every species of valuable right and interest including real and personal property, incorporeal hereditaments such as rents and services, rights of way, rights of profit or use in land of another, and choses in action ... [and to include] any tangible thing which the law protects under the name of property.[63]

Property even enjoys constitutional protection. Section 51(xxxi) states:

> 51. The Parliament shall, subject to this Constitution, have the power to make laws for the peace, order, and good government for the Commonwealth with respect to:
> (xxxi) The acquisition of property on just terms from any State or person for any purpose in respect of which the Parliament has the power to make laws.

In *WSGAL Pty Ltd v Trade Practices Commission*, the court held that the words 'for any purpose in respect of which the Parliament has the power to make laws' are not to be read as an exclusive or exhaustive statement of the Parliament's powers to deal with, or provide for, the involuntary disposition of or transfer of title to an interest in property. For there to be an acquisition of property by the Commonwealth, there must be an acquisition of an interest in property; this was given a broad definition to include 'slight or insubstantial interests'.[64] Given this tendency of the law, it would seem that future interpretations of Indigenous property should be interpreted in a way that acknowledges the vulnerability of the group to the abuse of power by the majority. Viewed against the protections given to property rights in the dominant legal system, native title is less valued, more vulnerable.

This is further evidenced by the need to exclude the operation of the *Racial Discrimination Act* 1975 (Cth) from certain aspects of the legislative scheme. The *First Report* of the Aboriginal and Torres Strait

---

63 *Minister of State for the Army v Dalziel* (1944) 68 CLR 261 at 290, per Starke J; 295 per McTiernan J.

64 *WSGAL Pty Ltd v Trade Practices Commission* (1994) ATPR ¶41-314 at 42,175-77, 42,585, 42,678.

Islander Social Justice Commissioner, then Mick Dodson, noted the following.

> Any interference with the Act which suspends, nullifies or reduces the rights of native title holders is, in itself, an act of racial discrimination. No people other than Aboriginal and Torres Strait Islander people would be adversely affected. It would adversely affect our enjoyment of equality before the law and our right to own property, inherit and not to be arbitrarily deprived of property. An equal right to enjoy natural justice, procedural fairness, which is conferred on native title holders through section 10 of the [Racial Discrimination] Act, would be removed.[65]

The Concluding Observations and Comments of the Convention to Eliminate all forms of Racial Discrimination (CERD) Committee reinforces this interpretation. It expressed concerns over the provisions of the *Native Title Act* 1993 (Cth) as amended, particularly the erosion of the right to negotiate and the exclusion of the consultation with Indigenous peoples in the development of the 10 Point Plan and the *Native Title Amendment Act* 1998 (Cth). The CERD Committee expressed concern about the compatibility of those provisions (particularly the 'validation' provisions, further extinguishment provisions, erosion of the right to negotiate and the primary production upgrade provisions) with Australia's obligations under the Convention, noting that:

> [w]hile the original 1993 Native Title Act was delicately balanced between the rights of indigenous and non-indigenous title-holders, the amended Act appears to create legal certainty for governments and third parties at the expense of indigenous titles.[66]

For a society in which all members were supposed to be equal under the law, an analysis of the way in which property rights have been treated with such different standards shows how the 'special measure' label is actually a euphemism for 'lesser protection'.

---

65 Aboriginal and Torres Strait Islander Social Justice Commission, 1993, p 23.
66 CERD/C/54/Misc40Rev2, para 6.

Different conceptions of equality

What the above examples highlight is the fact that 'same laws' for all Australians do not operate the same way for all Australians. Seemingly neutral laws can create disparate impacts that can strike hardest at the poorest, generally most disadvantaged members of the community: Indigenous peoples.

As the experience with native title shows, there is a deep historical context for this antagonism between the Indigenous community and the dominant Australian legal system. The British justified their 'settlement' of Australia under their own laws and international law. The legal fiction of *terra nullius* meant that the dominant culture's legal system was imposed in Australia at the time of the British invasion; no regard was had for the Indigenous legal system. The British legal system devalued Aboriginal laws, governance and culture and was based around the sole aim of empowering and enriching (in monetary terms) the British. These characteristics — the ignorance of Aboriginal law, the disrespect for Aboriginal culture and the hidden colonial ideology of the legal system — are evident in subsequent contact that Indigenous people have had with the justice system in Australia.

The law was not just the instrument by which the British claimed they had rightfully dispossessed Indigenous people. It was the instrument by which Indigenous people were kept on government reserves and deprived of basic human rights. It was the instrument that allowed the removal of Aboriginal children from their families as a part of a government policy of assimilation. In short, Indigenous people have always felt the power of the law, but rarely its protection.

Australian laws are, in most cases, based on a model of formal equality. The experience of Indigenous Australians shows that a seemingly neutral Constitution and criminal laws actually reproduce inherent discrimination and that property laws seen as 'special measures' are actually discriminatory and fashioned by colonial ideology. This bias is produced because institutions that are treated as being neutral are in fact entrenched in ideologies: property laws influenced by a national identity that allows the myth of *terra nullius* to remain; criminal laws that further the agenda of a neo-colonial state. By assuming that institutions are neutral, formal equality fails since it does not counter these entrenched ideologies and biases.

THE MYTH OF LAW'S NEUTRALITY

These three manifestations of law provide three different examples of how ideology can impact on the application of seemingly neutral laws.

- Values and ideologies can influence the way in which discretion is applied so that seemingly neutral laws are not applied neutrally at all.
- Values and ideologies can influence the way that law is interpreted if regard is had to the intention of the legislature in passing laws.
- There is the assumption that all people approach the law on an equal footing or level playing field.

This goes some way towards explaining why formal equality does not work for Indigenous Australians.

The experience of Indigenous claims to property rights, particularly post-*Mabo*, highlights the nationalistic rhetoric and ideology that is often infused into political and legal debates. Rather than mere historical imagery, nationalistic images can be manipulated in ways that profoundly affect the way that rights are seen and protected (or not). It also highlights the way in which perceptions and narratives of history fundamentally affect the way in which Australians see their nation and how they envision the type of society that Australia should become: views of history are profoundly linked to values.

A sense of identity is interwoven with views about history, law and society. It is reinforced by acknowledgement of that identity by oneself and by others. For this reason, and because experience is one of the keys to restructuring the relationship between Indigenous and non-Indigenous Australians, the next chapter will take a closer look at competing notions of nationalism that have shaped Australian values, laws and interpretations of history.

Chapter 3

Nationalism and identity: Why 'Western' institutions don't work for everyone

> To accept one's past – one's history – is not the same thing as drowning in it; it is learning how to use it. An invented past can never be used; it cracks and crumbles under the pressures of life like clay in a season of drought.[1]

Although it is impossible to define what it means to be Australian, their beliefs about the kind of society they are, the way they see themselves, the values they claim to embrace and their beliefs about what Australia 'ought' to be, reflect much about their attitudes and self-perceptions. Self-image influences one's values and ideas in a profound way, even when that image is a long way from reality. In this chapter, I want to explore some of the images that are projected of what it means to be Australian and look at research, particularly that of social researcher Hugh Mackay, that helps to articulate the way that Australians see themselves. An analysis of aspects of Australia's constructed nationalism will allow exploration of the way that a dominant identity generates an image that fosters 'sameness' and 'otherness', inclusion and exclusion, presence and absence.

Nationalist sentiment is challenged by Indigenous presence, perspective and experience. I want to consider examples of how Indigenous people challenge the dominant meta-narrative of Australian history, namely, the experiences of the Stolen Generations and experiences within the Australian education system.

---

1   J Baldwin, 1963, *The Fire Next Time*, Dial Press, p 71.

A question that also needs to be addressed concerns the importance of recognition. Why *do* acknowledgment and recognition seem to matter so much? Beginning to understand the importance of identity, community and recognition and why they are so valued allows consideration of the best ways to acknowledge and affirm these aspects of identity within a more inclusive society.

The Australian self-image

In the *Mackay Report: Being Australian: March 1988*,[2] a cross-section of Australians was interviewed to find their views on topics relating to their self-image and vision for Australia at the time of their country's bicentennial.

The *Mackay Report* confirmed a self-image of Australians and Australian life that has been threaded through Australian culture. According to Mackay, Australians see themselves as: masculine, sociable and friendly, spontaneous, fun-loving, having a sense of humour, versatile and resourceful, 'good sport' (both in sporting prowess and mateship), tough, resilient, popular and attractive, rural rather than urban, self-deprecating, down-to-earth.

Australians also see themselves as sceptical of authority, supportive of the hardworking family man, rugged and able to tame the harsh elements of the Australian landscape. These attributes lend themselves to images such as the 'little Aussie battler' (the hardworking, blue-collar worker or struggling farmer), sporting heroes, pioneers and the ANZACs. It is played out in the folklore of explorers, swagmen,[3] 'settlers' and farmers claiming, conquering and taming the Australian wilderness.

The glorification of the (male) working class struggler creates a culture that romanticises the unsung hero and the quiet achiever. It celebrates the underdog, 'the battler', struggling against adversity or higher, more powerful forces. These notions are reflected in the Australian aversion to the person who 'gets above himself'.

The nationalist sentiment has an anti-authoritarian aspect, an anti-intellectual aspect and an egalitarian aspect that derides 'tall

---

2   H Mackay, 1988, *Mackay Report: Being Australian: March 1988*, Mackay Research Centre for Communication Studies.
3   Men who travelled the country by foot, living off occasional work and carrying their belongings in a bundle, known as a swag.

poppies' and those who get above their station. This creates conflict between the romanticised notion of the (white) battler achieving against the odds and the anti-authoritarian, anti-intellectual ethos which disparages those who achieve too much or get 'too big for their boots'. Rise against adversity but don't achieve too much: a perfect recipe for mediocrity.

The romanticism of the working class man – be he worker or farmer – is linked to the dream that Australians have a sphere in which to act out this man-of-the-land, man-of-the-people fantasy. It is here that Australia's dream of home ownership is fostered and proprietorship over a small parcel of land becomes a fundamental aspect of Australian aspiration.

The nationalist self-image, like all forms of nationalism, is far from the realities of Australian life. Instead of being the man conquering the land or being the blonde, bronzed surf lifesaver, a study from the Australian Bureau of Statistics showed that Australians were in fact (predominantly urban) couch potatoes who spent most of their leisure time watching television, films, videos or computer screens.[4] Historian WG McMinn notes that at the time of Federation in Australia at the beginning of the 20th century, there was very little sense of an Australian nationalism.[5] Instead, Australians saw themselves as British subjects and were much more interested in their colonial cities. This indicates that the notion of an 'Australian' nationalism is a phenomenon of the (late) 20th century and that, as McMinn has observed, '[a]s realities fade, devotion to their symbols often becomes stronger.'[6]

The vision of Australia's future is divided. With an increasingly multicultural population mix, the aspirations of White Australia reflect an (imagined) Australia of the past. While Australian communities have seen an influx of people from all over the world who bring cultural practices and values with them that differ from the British-derived traditions of White Australia, many Australians are anxious about the rate of social change and fear that economic hardships and social dislocation may result.

---

4   Australian Bureau of Statistics, 1997b, *Cultural Trends in Australia*, Australian Government Printing Service.
5   WG McMinn, 1994, *Nationalism and Federalism in Australia*, Oxford University Press.
6   McMinn, 1994, p 306.

Resistance to developing multiculturalism within Australia especially comes from older Australians who grew up in the days of the White Australia policy and who link their identity with British heritage. Their views can be summed up in the recent statement by the President of the Victorian Returned Servicemens' League (RSL), Bruce Ruxton: 'Australia is a son of England and the mother country's beliefs and traditions are good enough for us.'[7] This view holds that the influx of immigrants, especially those from Asian countries, will jeopardise the Australia that now exists.

There is an emerging flip side to this that is reflected in the strong ground swell of support for the recognition of past injustice against Indigenous Australians. This was evident in the number of people and organisations, including many State parliaments, who apologised for the child removal practices after release of the *Bringing Them Home* report.[8] It was evidenced by the over 350,000 Australians who, on 28 May 2000, walked across the Sydney Harbour Bridge to show support for the reconciliation process. It was evidenced by the support for similar walks in Canberra and Melbourne, the number of people who signed 'Sorry Books' and who participated in the 'Sea of Hands'. This emerging strand of Australian consciousness may be more prevalent within younger generations than older, but it is led by a vast array of Australian people who feel a personal commitment to incorporating Indigenous perspectives and experiences into mainstream Australian society. The emergence of this newer strand which seeks reconciliation with Indigenous people as a high priority, reflects a rift between those who see Australia as 'a son of England' and those who seek a more diverse, inclusive and multicultural Australia.

Mary Kalantzis[9] describes the divide in national consciousness as consisting of the following characteristics: 'mainstream' versus 'noisy minority'; 'British' versus 'multicultural'; 'battler' versus 'feminist', 'Aboriginal' and 'ethnic'; 'heroic' versus 'black armband' views of history.

---

7   'Republicans, Bludgers and Hyenas – Ruxton Celebrates,' *Sydney Morning Herald*, 3 July 1997, p12.

8   HREOC, 1997.

9   Professor and Dean of the Faculty of Education, Language and Community Services, Royal Melbourne Institute of Technology.

This divide has been further highlighted by a denigration of multiculturalism and the disparaging of political correctness.[10]

Mackay noted in his book *Turning Point: Australians Choosing Their Future* that even though Australians are:

> overwhelmingly in favour of the multicultural ideal – Newspoll research showed that more than 70 per cent of us supported multiculturalism even at the height of Pauline Hanson's popularity – it is true that there are still many misgivings about it.[11]

He concluded that Australians are still not 'entirely comfortable with the theory of multiculturalism.'[12] They fear the changes it may bring and view it as a possible threat to the current way of life and to the mythical Australian culture.

An ideological struggle for Australia's future identity is taking place between an Australia locked into an embrace with the White Australia of the past and an Australia embracing the diverse and multicultural present. The conflict between these two views, these competing ideological visions of Australia, comes to the fore in any debate that raises issues of Australian identity: whether Australia becomes a Republic, what is appropriate for inclusion in a Preamble to the Australian Constitution, Australia's role in international conflict and its reputation upon the world stage.

Australia's racist nationalism: The perceived threat of 'the other'

People bond when they have a common enemy; constructing demons who threaten a certain way of life will unite people against those threats. Australia's nationalism has a xenophobic streak which has focused its wrath on several groups seen as threatening, as 'other', to the conservative, historically dominant vision of White Australia. These are the catch-all groups of Asians, Indigenous people and, more recently, Muslims.

---

10 Paper delivered by Mary Kalantzis at *Unchain My Mind: New Social-Democratic Ideas for Labor in Government*, 27 July 2000, Trades Hall, Melbourne.

11 H Mackay, 1999, *Turning Point: Australian's Choosing Their Future*, Macmillan, p 40.

12 Mackay, 1999, p 35.

The *Mackay Report* highlighted the extent to which anti-Asian sentiment was still part of the Australian psyche. With its findings that Australia has a strong anti-Asian undercurrent, it predicted the support for populist member of Parliament, Pauline Hanson. Hanson was pre-selected by the Liberal Party but was disendorsed when she made anti-Asian statements. Yet, her racist and xenophobic attitudes gained her public support from some sectors of the Australian community. She ran as an independent candidate in the 1996 federal election and was subsequently elected to the Commonwealth Parliament.

The emergence of Pauline Hanson's populist politics was seen by many as an anomaly, especially by those in the traditionally less conservative urban areas of Australia,. Yet Hanson had tapped into something within the consciousness of many Australians. Prime Minister John Howard initially refused to counter the extremist and xenophobic views of Hanson, as though fearful that he would alienate his own electorate. The capturing of xenophobic sentiment is arguably what put Howard into government for a third term in 2001 as he harnessed the populist rhetoric of keeping boat people (primarily Muslims) out of Australia and using tough measures to thwart their attempts to arrive in Australia and seek refugee status.

In *Turning Points*, Mackay took a reflective look at this xenophobia. He concluded that although the rise of Pauline Hanson's One Nation party was a sign of deep disquiet in the body politic and support for Hanson was based partly on classic xenophobia, the emergence of One Nation forced Australians to 'reconsider our view of multiculturalism and to decide that we like it, warts and all.'[13] Mackay pinpointed 'the effects of 25 years of relentless change – cultural, social, economic, technological' as the source of the discontent that gave rise to the insecurities that drive people to nurture some of their darkest phobias – most particularly, xenophobia.[14] At such moments, ethnic minorities will always be vulnerable to people looking for scapegoats.

The 'otherness' of Indigenous people in Australia

Although from 500 different groups, Indigenous people from diverse cultural groups remain politically united against the dominant culture

---

13   Mackay, 1999, p 280.
14   Mackay, 1999, p 282.

through their ongoing struggle to come to terms with the continuing colonisation processes. Despite a diverse cultural make-up, Indigenous people in contemporary Australian society are often perceived in one of two ways: as relics of the past; or, especially if less than 'full-blood', as inauthentic and devoid of culture.

The romanticised notion that Indigenous people are a relic of the past leads to the idea of the 'Aborigine' as a 'noble savage'. Take, for example, this view in *Wonderful Australia in Pictures*.

> Such are the Australians – the original Australians. A kindly, gentle and patient people, they are heirs to an ancient culture which the white takes from them, giving nothing in return. They are self-reliant, observant (their fame as trackers is notable and deserved), frank, open and fond of laughter ... The Australian aboriginal is a slowly vanishing relic of an age that is so long gone that it is lost behind the thick mists of history.[15]

and

> In many respects the aboriginal natives are the most astonishing of all Australia's curiosities, for in the atomic age of man's greatest discoveries this lost race remains in an apparent state of arrested development, held like living fossils in the museum of time.[16]

Australian stereotypes of Indigenous people reflect colonial attitudes and deeply entrenched racism. Indigenous people tend to be characterised either as troublemakers or as those who tow the line. The 'good ones' assimilate or keep to themselves; the 'bad ones' are activists who seek to assert their rights. Consider the backlash against runner Cathy Freeman when she, in a candid, personal interview, offered her reflections on the way that the removal policy had impacted on her family and her feelings about the government's response to the *Bringing Them Home* report. Freeman's observations about her own family and her own life were seen as highly political and led to the following attitude: 'What a pity Cathy Freeman had chosen to be embroiled in the racist debate. Hitherto she has been a splendid sporting ambassador for Australians.'[17] Speaking out made her the object of hostility. Again, this attitude towards Indigenous

---

15 The Sun News-Pictorial, 1949, *Wonderful Australia in Pictures*, Herald and Weekly Times, p 129.
16 The Sun News-Pictorial, 1949, p 119.
17 W Pike, 2000, Letter to the Editor, *Sydney Morning Herald*, 19 July.

people was identified in the *Mackay Report*: 'Some of them are top blokes, but most of them don't seem to be too happy to do things our way.'[18]

Many Australians, unaware of historical context, decontextualise the socio-economic problems faced by Australia's Indigenous population. They perceive Indigenous people as being from a traditional, 'primitive' culture, or only see their contemporary impoverished situation. Without the awareness of how genocide, dispossession, cultural genocide, and discrimination have created a legacy of cyclical poverty (and a lack of secure rights in relation to property interests), some Australians view the position of Indigenous people at the lowest level of Australian society as being solely their own fault. They erroneously assume that Indigenous people are on a level playing field with all other Australians.

> Every other race that has come to this country has had problems. We have all come in with some kind of opposition and difficulty. But we all stand and do our best and we are all Australians now. We are all one. That's the way that Aborigines have to look at it too.[19]

In fact, many Australians believe that they are more than fair in their treatment of Indigenous people and remain suspicious of the legitimacy of claims to land. They have a firm belief that Indigenous people should not be singled out for special treatment.

> If other people had settled here, the Aborigines might have got a much rougher deal than they got from the Brits. From one point of view, they are quite lucky that it's us who came here, and not someone who would have been much harder to get on with.[20]

Belief in the myth of the British coming to Australia and taming its mysteries avoids asking questions about the vanishing Indigenous population and the validity and morality of British claims to property and sovereignty. In recent years, there has been an increased awareness of aspects of the experience of Aboriginal people in Australian society. The RCIADIC's *National Report* and the HREOC'S *Bringing Them Home* report on the practice of removing Indigenous children from their families and communities and the subsequent impact of these practices has brought public attention to issues of which many

---

18 Mackay, 1988, p 44.
19 Mackay, 1988, p 44.
20 Mackay, 1988, p 46.

Australians had previously been ignorant. Yet even in the face of evidence of historical injustices and their continued legacies, Australians in many quarters seem tenaciously resistant to the idea that they should formally acknowledge the treatment of Indigenous people at the hands of the settlers and subsequent government policies. While some Australians are prepared to face some historical facts, other Australians are not prepared to think about how these realities undermine the national self-image, nor the extent to which these myths have created an institutional legacy.

This sentiment was reflected in comments made by Prime Minister John Howard after the report on the removal of Indigenous children was made public.

> So far as the public is concerned, they don't believe in intergenerational guilt and they do believe that this country has a proud history ... Some of the past practices, although they might be condemned now, were done with the best motives and intentions and many people were in fact cared for in warm and loving homes.[21]

Political commentators were quick to note that the Prime Minister was trying to target a perceived public opinion about the way in which 'mainstream' Australians wish to deal with their past.[22]

Political scientist AF Davies has explored the notion of guilt in Australian society. Davies understood that guilt could be used in trying to avoid repetition of what had already caused remorse. He noted that there was a denial of obligation to Indigenous Australians and there was a projection of blame onto Indigenous people in order to deflect it from the actions of white Australians and their ancestors. Davies recognised that this ideology fabricated a righteous aggression. He believed that the notion of collective guilt was made up of 'the sum of individual guilt which was projected onto others and resulted in scapegoating'.[23]

Social researcher Hugh Mackay notes the tendency for Indigenous people to be overlooked and forgotten; for example, when people speak of 'traditional Australian values', they do not apply those values to Indigenous people.

---

21 'Why we can't sleep soundly', *Sydney Morning Herald*, 28 May 1997, p 17.
22 Ibid.
23 AF Davies, 1988, *Three Essays in Political Psychology*, McPhee Gribble, Penguin Books, p 80.

When they talk about religious freedom, they rarely include Aboriginal religious life in their discussions. When they talk about the attractive diversity of Australian life – and the ability of Australians to choose their styles of living – they rarely acknowledge the diversity of Aboriginal people and the complexity of *their* different ways of life.[24]

A Newspoll survey undertaken in 2000 showed the conflicting attitudes many Australians have to Indigenous people.[25] According to that research, 80 per cent saw Indigenous people as treated unfairly and harshly in the past while only 41 per cent considered them to be a disadvantaged group today. Eighty per cent thought that there had been enough talk of how Indigenous people were treated in the past and that 'we should concentrate on the future.'[26] While 70 per cent acknowledged the need for government initiatives to reduce Indigenous disadvantage, 60 per cent also thought that Indigenous people received too much government assistance. As the researchers concluded:

> If it is a statistical fact that Aboriginal and Torres Strait Islander people are the poorest, unhealthiest, least employed, worst housed and most imprisoned Australians, but only half the community believes Aboriginal people are worse off than other Australians (only around 30 per cent believe they are 'a lot' worse off), then there is a significant gap between the facts and what many people believe about the position of Aboriginal people.[27]

The above research was further reinforced by a Saulwick and Muller qualitative study that found:

- There is a willingness to treat Indigenous Australians like any other Australians, provided they are prepared to accept 'Australian' values and 'Australian' rules.
- There is a level of impatience with, and lack of understanding of, Indigenous people who do not conform with 'general community norms'.
- Indigenous people living in cities are believed not to be 'real' Indigenous people, particularly if they are not 'full-bloods; instead

---

24 Mackay, 1999, p 125.
25 Reprinted in Grattan, 2000, p 33.
26 Grattan, 2000, p 34.
27 Grattan, 2000, p 34.

it is believed that they are claiming Aboriginality in order to gain welfare benefits.
- There is a vehement belief that past actions cannot be judged by present standards.
- The majority felt that they should not take responsibility for past actions, nor did they feel the need to apologise for past actions.

From these findings, the study concluded:
- Behind the responses lay an intolerance, a lack of empathy and an inability or disinclination to look at the matter from an Indigenous perspective
- Respondents who had grown up with Indigenous people and who had Indigenous friends tended to view Indigenous people in a negative stereotypical manner.[28]

With these attitudes so prevalent, it is easier to see how the myth of *terra nullius* was allowed to exist in Australian law up until 1992 and in the Australian psyche to the present day. It is easier to understand why efforts to assert Indigenous claims to land are so vehemently resisted.

Subscribing to the belief that Australia was vacant at the time of European arrival means it is easier for Indigenous people to remain invisible, meaning it is also easier to keep nationalist myths and self-images intact.

It is often argued that romanticised myths are harmless, but Hugh Mackay, in talking about the rural myth, notes two reasons why a tenacious embrace of myth can weaken us.
- First, we don't adapt – emotionally – to the reality of life: by clinging to the rural myth, we increase our sense of restlessness and dissatisfaction with the reality of urban living and we don't cope with it as well as we might if we embraced it more realistically as a legitimately Australian way of life.[29]
- Secondly, we find it difficult to face the bleak truth about rural Australia and its problems. The myth of the bush pioneer, the flinty, resourceful, sardonic, laconic stockman who can cope with

---

28 Grattan, 2000, pp 36–9.
29 Mackay, 1999, p 44.

anything blinds us to the harsh realities of life in the bush, and to the special needs of rural communities.[30]

There is a third reason: the general acceptance of myth as reality can affect those people who fall outside or challenge those myths. This is true of many sectors of Australian society – women, migrants, gays and lesbians – but none more so than Indigenous Australians. It can influence the way 'neutral laws' are interpreted and applied, creating unequal outcomes, and it can infuse seemingly neutral institutions with ideologies. For these reasons, it is inevitable that the laws and institutions of society are constructed with the values of the dominant culture and that they produce unsatisfactory results, conflict, marginalisation and ostracism for those who find themselves challenging those values. This goes some way towards explaining why 'Western' institutions often fail Indigenous people. At the same time, it also provides an explanation of why the presence of Indigenous people and their experiences and history can be so confronting to members of the dominant culture who embrace the imperialistic and colonial narratives of Australian history.

Challenging the Australian self-image

Two areas assist in understanding how experiences have fundamentally differed for immigrant Australians and Indigenous Australians: the effect of the Aborigines Protection Board on Indigenous families and Indigenous identity; and the discrimination within and access to services such as education.

Far from being just historical practices and policies of the Australian government, the policies of conquest, dispossession and assimilation remain part of the reality for Indigenous people today. These two areas provide an historical context in which to understand contemporary Indigenous society, showing how life today is deeply entrenched with the legacy of colonial ideologies.

The Aborigines Protection Board in NSW

Every State and Territory in Australia had an Aborigines Protection Board or equivalent regime. The Board set up in NSW serves as a case-in-point with resonance in all jurisdictions.

---

30 Mackay, 1999, p 4-5.

In 1909, the NSW government passed the *Aborigines Protection Act 1909* (NSW), giving a legislative basis to the Aborigines Protection Board. At first, the Board only had the power to remove children from their families if they were considered to be neglected. These powers were broadened beyond circumstances of abuse and neglect in 1919, allowing the Board to pursue a policy of assimilation. However, the Board had begun removing as many children as it could by 1915. Each State and Territory had an equivalent statute.

The colour of a child's skin determined how the state would determine that child's future (highlighting the racist aspects of this policy). Fairer-skinned Indigenous children were more likely to be adopted into white families. Darker-skinned children were more likely to be institutionalised or sent out to work. Fairer-skinned children also tended to be removed at younger ages than darker-skinned children. Though some like to emphasise that these policies were made with the best of intentions, there is clear evidence that racist attitudes also motivated the practice *and*, at the time, non-Indigenous Australians thought it was wrong.

The *Bringing Them Home* report helped to dispel the myth that children were 'rescued' for welfare reasons. When an official document lists the reason for the Board taking the child as 'For Being Aboriginal', the chief motivation becomes clear.

Many Protection Board documents have been destroyed, effectively dislocating Indigenous children who were too young to remember where their people were from or where their families and ancestral lands are. Children that were taken away were not taught their own stories by Indigenous Elders. Instead, they were taught the white culture and the white system. They were taught that they were inferior and that their culture was inferior. If children did not have a strong cultural background, they tended to be persuaded by the cultural propaganda preached within the institutions they were confined to, or by the families into which they were adopted. The policy of re-socialisation was a form of cultural genocide.

The legislative power to remove Indigenous children remained until 1969, though the practice continued informally after that date. The legacies remain. Indigenous communities are riddled with suicide, mental problems, substance abuse, family breakdown and cycles of poverty, all of which can often be traced back to removal policies of the Aborigines Protection Board. There was not one Indigenous family in NSW that was not affected by the practices of the Board. A 1994 survey showed that one in ten persons aged 25 years and over had been separated from their family during childhood.[31] Today a new generation of Indigenous children find themselves in families where breakdowns have become cyclical.

Two-thirds of the people whose deaths were investigated by the RCIADIC had been removed from their families as children. In his *Report of the Inquiry into the Death of Malcolm Charles Smith*, Commissioner Wootten noted the removal policy's 'catastrophic effects on [Malcolm Smith's] life and ultimately his death.'[32] Citing the National Aboriginal and Islander Legal Services Secretariat (NAILSS), the report added:

> the survivors of Kinchela (and Cootamundra Girls Home) and their children are now adults, struggling against the odds to lead normal lives in a world that is permanently disordered from the inside out. An indeterminate number find themselves in a revolving door relationship with police, hospitals, prisons and various debilitating dependencies. Malcolm Smith was one of many.[33]

The report goes on to add '[c]onstantly one meets people whose lives have been shattered or gravely disturbed by the taking away of children ... There are many heart rending stories of searches and reunions in the Aboriginal community.'[34]

It was this legacy that the *Bringing them Home* report sought to investigate. It attempted to identify the effects of the policy on those whose life it shattered. It catalogued the effects on the child, including:

- the effects of separation from the primary carer;
- the effects of institutionalisation;
- the effects of abuses and denigration, including those of sexual abuse, physical abuse and racism;
- the effects of separation from the Indigenous community, including loss of cultural knowledge and struggles with Indigenous identity;

---

31 Richard Madden, 1995, *National Aboriginal and Torres Strait Islander Survey 1994*, AGPS, p 2.
32 Royal Commission into Aboriginal Deaths in Custody (RCIADIC), 1989, *Report of the Inquiry into the Death of Malcolm Charles Smith*, Australian Government Publishing Service, p 73.
33 RCIADIC, 1989, p 74.
34 RCIADIC, 1989, p 74.

ACHIEVING SOCIAL JUSTICE

- the effects on families and communities who lost children;
- the intergenerational effects such as parenting problems, behavioural problems, violence, unresolved grief and mental illness.

The report is peppered with oral histories. Just two will give a sense of how hard it is to quantify these experiences.

> Eric is brought easily to tears as he recalls the events of his life ... When speaking of members of his family he feels a great emotional pain, that in fact he doesn't believe that there is anyone left close to him, he feels as if he has been deprived of contact with his mother and his siblings by the separation at a young age and he feels acutely the pain of his brother's death in custody.[35]
>
> I didn't know any Aboriginal people at all – none at all. I was placed in a white family and I was just – I was white, I never knew, I never accepted myself to being a black person until – I don't know – I don't know if you ever really do accept yourself as being ... How can you be proud of being Aboriginal after all the humiliation and the anger and the hatred you have? It's unbelievable how much you can hold inside.[36]

Despite the broad reaching and long-lasting effects of the policy on Indigenous families across the continent, Australian history says little of the activities of the Protection Boards. Many Australians did not even know that the Boards existed until the controversy over the *Bringing Them Home* report, even though there has been an extensive collection of the oral histories of Indigenous people who, as children, experienced life under the 'care' of the Boards.

Despite the clear links that the report made between past government practices and the contemporary legacies of cyclical family breakdown, substance abuse, mental health problems and suicide, the Federal Government has sought to minimise and even deny these links. The Federal Government's stance encourages misperceptions from some sections of the population. Consider the following, again in response to Cathy Freeman's expression of how the removal policy affected her family. 'If Cathy Freeman's grandmother had not been rescued she may not have survived and Cathy may never have been born. Think about it Cathy, and all those who support the "stolen generations" myth.'[37]

---

35 HREOC, 1997, p 179.
36 HREOC, 1997, p 200.
37 M Wilson, 2000, Letter to the Editor, *Sydney Morning Herald*, 19 July.

What is apparent here is an automatic assumption that the removal was motivated by bad parenting and for the child's own good. There is a trivialisation of the effect of the action on generations of Freeman's family. There is ignorance of the fact that children were taken because of their race and not for welfare reasons. The author of this quote seems unable to acknowledge the ideologies of assimilation and breeding out that drove the policy and is insensitive to the fact that Freeman expresses an event that caused her and her family much grief and sadness. Instead, this expression of hurt is met with the response that it was for her own good.

The *Bringing Them Home* report divided Australians between those who sought to trivialise the report and the experiences it highlighted and those who sought reconciliation. Contrast the response of Prime Minister John Howard ('Australians of this generation should not be required to accept guilt and blame for past actions and policies over which they have no control')[38] with that of Governor-General William Deane ('It is vital that we acknowledge past injustices and recognise wounds inflicted by our earlier policy of denial').[39] One reflects on history as a construct and the other of history as a lesson. Howard's response speaks of the effects of colonisation as a phenomenon of the past. Deane's response goes some way towards acknowledging that the ideologies of colonisation are inherent in the institutions of society by recognising that past government policies are having a profound effect on the lives of Indigenous people today.

Discrimination in the education system

The Australian education system has perpetuated the colonial ideologies of Australian society and reinforced its nationalist identity in two ways:

- by denying access to, and thus disempowering, Indigenous Australians; and
- by indoctrinating Australian children into a particular conception of their own history and a particular nationalist vision.

---

38 'Mr Howard unreconciled', *Sydney Morning Herald*, 27 May 1997, p 14.
39 'Governor calls for 'recognition', *Sydney Morning Herald*, 3 June 1997, p 5.

Exclusion

The policies of the Aborigines Protection Boards meant that Indigenous children provided a pool of cheap, unskilled labour. Aboriginal and Torres Strait Islander children were taught on the missions and reserves but the levels of education were never very high. When children were removed from their families, they were sent to institutions where they were taught until their early teens and then sent to white families to do domestic work or to work as stockmen. Indigenous children were treated as unteachable and not educated past the age of 14, no matter how well they were doing at school.

Indigenous people have fought hard to gain access to educational institutions, as they know only too well what the effects of lack of access to education are. Instead of helping advance the situation of the Indigenous population, education was used by governments as a way of eliminating traditional Indigenous values and to further implement the policy of assimilation.

Today, participation levels of Indigenous people in the school system are increasing but remain much lower than the national average. At the time of the RCIADIC reports in 1991, 7.5 per cent of Indigenous people over 18 had never been to school. Participation rates in secondary schools are increasing. But by the mid-1990s, only 19.4 per cent of Indigenous students completed the final year of high school, compared to 53.1 per cent of non-Aboriginal students. Few Indigenous students who complete their secondary education have the level of results needed to enter university. The high school retention rates for Indigenous students is 25.2 per cent, compared with 77 per cent for all Australians. Further, 90 per cent of school-age Indigenous teenagers in remote desert communities have the reading and writing skills of 7 year olds.[40] Nearly half of the Indigenous population aged 15 and over had no formal training or had not reached 10-year-old levels.[41]

These statistics hint at, but perhaps do not properly explain, the impact of the exclusion of Indigenous people. In the RCIADIC *Report of the Inquiry into the Death of Harrison Day*, Commissioner Wootten noted the importance of education for Indigenous people.

---

40 'Literary crisis for outback Aborigines', *Sydney Morning Herald*, 19 October 1996, p 13.
41 Ibid.

> [I]t is of the utmost urgency to ensure that education is effectively delivered to Aboriginals. Otherwise, we face the future of growing numbers of Aboriginals, who, like Harrison Day, find themselves without the education or skills to pursue any work other than that which is rapidly becoming obsolete in an increasingly technological society.[42]

Commissioner Wootten went on to note the problems in relation to education that had been brought to his attention during the period of the Commission's investigations.

> [T]oo few examples of worthwhile positions being open to Aboriginals who persist with education; parents who themselves had no educational opportunities and do not always appreciate the needs of student children or the value of education; houses which are overcrowded and households which include heavy drinkers and provide little opportunity for children to study or even to present themselves at school ready for a day's work; teachers who do not understand these problems and punish Aboriginal children for matters beyond their control; and curricula that ignore and discourage Aboriginal culture and achievement ... The teaching of Aboriginal children is not taken seriously, absences are not followed up, children are promoted on the basis of age rather than readiness, and then encouraged simply to keep quiet until leaving age and then leave.[43]

Commissioner Wootten identifies a history of exclusion and a cyclical poverty that has not allowed Indigenous people to enjoy access to education to the same extent as other Australians. However, physical exclusion from school is only one part of the problem with the education system and its treatment of Indigenous people. As Wootten alluded to, there is also an ideological exclusion.

Indoctrination

Indigenous culture has existed on Australian soil for at least 40,000 years. Traditional Indigenous culture, the impact of colonisation on Indigenous communities and the realities of their modern lives remain a mystery to most Australians. Information about Indigenous culture or post-invasion experience is not taught in schools – with the

---

42 Royal Commission into Aboriginal Deaths in Custody (RCIADIC), 1990, *Report of the Inquiry into the Death of Harrison Day*, Australian Government Publishing Service, p 59.
43 RCIADIC, 1990, p 59.

exception of cursory explanations of Indigenous hunting tools, eating habits and Dreamtime stories. The intricacies of Indigenous culture – the concept of family, the way that Indigenous people see themselves in relation to the rest of the world and their social and legal structures – are ignored. Historical and contemporary experiences of genocidal practices and institutional racism were, until recently, kept from school curricula.

Bill Cope undertook an empirical study of 630 texts used in Australian schools from 1945 to 1985. He noted a change in school texts from 1960, and a

> move away from an old story of Australia in which history is a narrative of progress and development, with cultural differences conceived as a matter of superiority/inferiority; dominance and suppression of other cultures is depicted as a historical necessity, as, for example, in the assimilation of Aborigines and immigrants to the structural and technical movement of an ever-modernising industrialism.[44]

Despite the fact that texts now supposedly celebrate cultural difference, historical perspective can be biased. Cope's study extracts the following from a textbook with a circulation of well over 200,000 copies written by Russel Ward, who wrote *The Australian Legend* (1966).

> There are still living today in Arnhem Land people who know almost no history. They are Aboriginal tribesmen who live in practically the same way as their forefathers and ours did, tens of thousands of years ago. Like them they have not only no accurate knowledge of past events, but no aeroplanes, motor-cars or picture shows; not even any books, houses or clothes. Apart from the fact that they use weapons of stone and wood to hunt for their food, their lives are almost as hard and as dangerous as those of the animals, who also hunt to live ... [W]e are civilized today and they are not. History helps us to understand why this is so.

Cope warned that:

> this sort of multicultural education can inadvertently provide grist for the racist mill, immersing children in colourful differences during 'national days', for example, but really exaggerating and constructing stereotypes of cultural difference in order to celebrate them.[45]

---

44 B Cope, 1987, *Racism, Popular Culture and Australian Identity in Transition: a Case Study of Change in School Textbooks Since 1945*, Common Ground, p 1.

45 Cope, 1987, p 7.

History curriculum remains a battleground in the ideological struggle between the vision of a white Australia and the more contemporary vision of a multicultural or cosmopolitan Australia.

The following statement by the Prime Minister John Howard reflects the reluctance of some Australians to understand and acknowledge the real history of their country.

> Of course we treated the Aboriginals very, very badly in the past ... but to tell children whose parents were no part of that maltreatment, to tell children who themselves have been no part of it, that we're all part of a sort of racist and bigoted history is something that Australians reject.[46]

David Hollinsworth, author and senior lecturer at the University of South Australia, responded to the Prime Minister's comments.

> Part of the job of a teacher is to teach people how to understand the past and critically understand the present through this. It is important not to wallow around on a guilt trip – that does no good at all. But it is even more important not to censor history.[47]

As Hollinsworth points out, revising Australia's past is not about generating guilt, it is about generating understanding. In their book *Telling the Truth About History*, Joyce Appleby, Lynn Hunt and Margaret Jacob conclude:

> What you do not know can be hurtful because it denies you a better informed conception of reality. History offers tools for liberation. History teaches that members of society build structures but also transform them ... Telling the truth takes a collective effort.[48]

The ability to *understand* history allows lessons to be learned rather than fantasies to continue. A distorted history creates a distorted national image and romanticising history to promote a fictitious national image helps no one. Members of the dominant culture chain their children to a legacy of ignorance while Indigenous people are denied the dignity of acknowledgment, let alone apology, for what has happened to them and their families.

---

46 'History, white or wrong?', *Sydney Morning Herald*, 26 October 1996, p 33.
47 Ibid.
48 J Appleby, L Hunt and M Jacob, 1994, *Telling the Truth About History*, WW Norton, p 309.

The silence within Australia's education system regarding the history of their country and the treatment of Indigenous people leaves many Australians unable to understand the contemporary impact of past practices and the extent to which they permeate contemporary institutions. A vast number of Australians do not know any Indigenous people, do not mix with Indigenous people socially; they rarely live within Indigenous communities, whether rural or urban. This lack of contact, coupled with a lack of education about experiences and perspectives, allows Indigenous communities to become invisible, appearing only to fill negative (or positive) stereotypes.

The use of history to prop up a constructed national identity perpetuates an obstacle for reconciliation between all sectors of Australian society. The decontextualisation fractures Australian society, creating tensions between competing understandings of what Australia is and competing visions of what Australia should be.

Why recognition matters:
The importance of community and identity

The tensions between Indigenous Australians and the dominant culture are wrapped up in identity: how Australians see themselves, how they see others and how they want society to respect who they are. Personal identity is formed not only through their internal distinctiveness but through their experience with others and the stereotypes society lays before them. It is shaped by self-expression and through their interaction with others, their socialisation by family, education and community and their positive and negative experience in the world.

Who we are is a process. We develop as we go along, transformed by our intellectual, emotional and spiritual growth, moulded by the actions, judgments and expectations of others. How societies deal with 'otherness' and 'sameness' will impact on their ability to allow individuals freedom from oppression and enough scope for the exercise of liberty. Our identity thus has two dimensions to it.

- A *personal* internal aspect (narcissistic, introverted and existential) that needs space and freedom for self-expression.
- A *communal* external aspect (communal, extroverted and fraternal) that needs public space and institutional arrangements that allow respect for others and the space and freedom to do as they wish.

The experience of Indigenous people, their tenacity in claiming Indigenous cultural identity in the face of racist and assimilationist policies, is testament to the fundamental and central role identity plays in their lives. Charles Taylor refers to the core of our self – our 'authentic self' – in the following way.

> There is a certain way of being human that is *my* way. I am called upon to live my life this way, and not in imitation of anyone else's life. But this notion gives a new importance to being true to myself. If I am not, I miss the point of my life.[49]

This need to 'live my life this way', this desire to be 'what I can and what I want', is embodied in the notion of personal liberty. Adherence to a principle of personal liberty can foster the environment in which self-expression is possible.

John Stuart Mill understood the communal context for the realisation of personal liberty.

> It is not by wearing down into uniformity all that is individual in themselves, but by cultivating it and calling it forth, within the limits imposed by the rights and interests of others, that human beings become a noble and beautiful object of contemplation; and as the works partake the character of those who do them, by the same process human life also becomes rich, diversified, and animating, furnishing more abundant aliment to high thoughts and elevating feelings, and strengthening the tie that binds every individual to the race, by making the race infinitely better worth belonging to.[50]

Mill offers an acknowledgment of the importance of allowing people to have the space in which to explore their authentic self. Mill believed that this should be done through the fostering of difference, that we should only be constrained by our actions to the extent to which they harm others.

People need space within the societies in which they live to be able to express their identity and difference. It is when this 'difference' is silenced that tension, antagonism and conflict begin. The need to have space in which to recognise this difference is crucial and is appreciated as a fundamental right, consistent with and central to the

---

49 C Taylor, 1994, *Multiculturalism: Examining the politics of recognition*, Princeton University Press, p 29.
50 JS Mill, 1993 (first published 1859), *On Liberty and Utilitarianism*, Bantam Books, p 72.

notion of personal liberty. The notion of individual freedom recognises the importance of ensuring dignity by protecting the fundamental aspects of the self. It means recognising that each person has complex ideas, personal preferences and ways of identifying and, as such, needs to have their personal and group affiliations recognised and protected. Cultural practices, religious beliefs, sexual preference and gender all form pieces of a complex puzzle that metamorphose into the identity of an individual. The dignity of a person, any person, is tied to respect for those differences, regardless of whether we embrace the same values or not.

This desire for individual freedom to allow full expression of the authentic self needs to be placed in a communal context. Liberal philosophy includes an inherent belief in the principle of mutual respect, coupled with an understanding of the interdependence of human relations. A communal aspect arises in various relationships to the self, for example:

- through *socialisation* through cultural and religious practices within a group;
- through *experience* outside of the socialising group;
- through *affirmation* through the communal validation of the self; and
- through *choice* to pursue individual personal freedom through interdependent relationships.

The relationship between the individual and the group is complex, multi-layered and multi-faceted. Group identity is an intricate part of personal identity. We need to be able to freely interact with our communities and be given the broadest ability to follow cultural practices and observe cultural beliefs. Community becomes important in two ways:

- it generates resistance through the creation of feelings of 'otherness' (it acts as a reflector); and
- it validates through the generation of feelings of 'sameness' (it acts as a validator).

Communitarians argue that the liberal view of the 'self' is empty, ignores our need for communal practices, overlooks the need for social confirmation of our individual judgments and pretends to have an impossible universality or objectiveness. This acknowledgment of the importance of allowing individuals space – both privately and publicly – to express choices and differences is enriched by understanding the importance of a communal context.

Not only does an individual need access to community for integrity and self-expression but these same individuals also *choose* to live with social arrangements that are interdependent. We have a natural inclination to join groups and align ourselves with others. Our sense of who we are is reinforced by life choices that seek reciprocity, kinship and union. We choose to enter into these relationships and obligations to enrich our notion of a free and independent self.

In the case of Indigenous people, the complexities of identity and self-expression are intertwined with the protection of Indigenous rights. Discrimination based on race pushes identity to the forefront of life experience. It defines an Indigenous person as an outsider – the 'other' – and creates a bond with others who have similar experiences and ties.

This leads to complex self-identification which other Australians have difficulty understanding: Why is it that a person who lives in the urban areas of Australia is so adamant about being identified and respected for their Aboriginality? Why is the protection and recognition of identity the central core of Indigenous political claims, wrapped in every political notion from Indigenous property rights to the right to equality to the notion of sovereignty?

When laws prohibit Indigenous people from attending school, or when the expressions of Australian nationalism remain silent about their existence, Aboriginality is brought to the forefront of their experience. Trivialising the importance of the identity of Indigenous peoples (and the cultural practices and colonial experiences which helped shape it) denigrates Indigenous people, ignoring, excluding and demeaning their experience. A societal structure that seeks to ignore, or to threaten, aspects of the self can cause an individual to react; it can cause a person to feel that identification even more.

Indigenous people share a cultural heritage but they also share the experience of colonisation. These shared experiences (socialisation, heritage, history) validate and provide an enclave of inclusion and solidarity, detached from the wider community. These experiences – both negative as a result to discrimination and poor self-image and positive due to the re-affirmation of the Indigenous community and the pride in their history and cultural heritage – become defining aspects of Indigenous self-identity.

In this way, identity is not just created by what an individual wants to emphasise but also by what society emphasises about the individual. This includes cultural differences, religious differences, gender differences and differences in sexual preference. It is not every aspect that demands political space – brown eyes, brown hair, or liking 80s music or enjoying kickboxing, for example – but instead those that society seems most ready to identify, distinguish, attack or suppress.

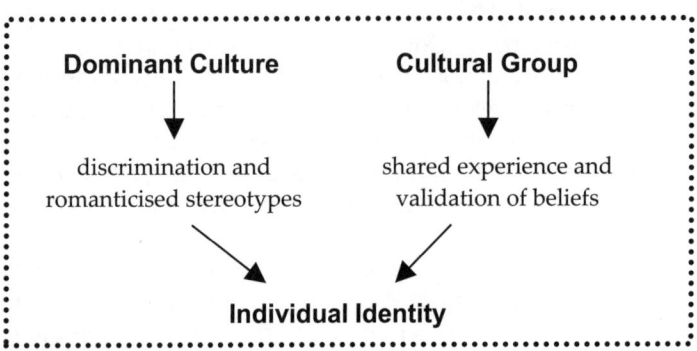

Many people fear that the recognition of different cultures within a multicultural society will undermine the cultural life of the dominant or homogenised culture. This fear is misplaced, as acknowledgment and recognition of other cultures can be enriching for societies; multiculturalism promotes diversity and creates alternative institutional options. Other cultures offer different value systems, different technology, different approaches to problem solving, different understandings of the way the world works and different ways of being. Just as Indigenous cultures are developing with the contact they have had with colonising nations, dominant cultures can be enriched by their contact with 'outsiders'. Martha Minow, a professor of law at Harvard University, who specialises in the impact of law on minorities, offers three reasons why a majority culture not composed of traditional 'sub-cultures' should be interested in preserving cultural identity and diversity:

- they provide settings in which individuals can develop sense of self through common history and commitment;
- they provide a check against an absolute authority structure that could suppress the alternatives; and

- tolerance and equality depends on preservation of differences that could become subject to tolerance and equal treatment.[51]

In democratic societies, the co-existence of diversity with equal rights means ensuring every citizen has the opportunity to grow up within their cultural heritage and to have his or her children grow up within it without suffering discrimination because of their cultural affiliation or race. Diversity also provides each person a wider choice of possibilities for the expression of personal liberty and self-expression.

Charles Taylor, Emeritus Professor of Philosophy at McGill University, identifies two kinds of dominantly employed variants of liberalism that seek to promote this personal liberty and self-expression.

- *treating all people equally*: ie, 'difference-blind', 'neutral'; and
- recognising difference and fostering the expression of difference, ie, 'multicultural'.

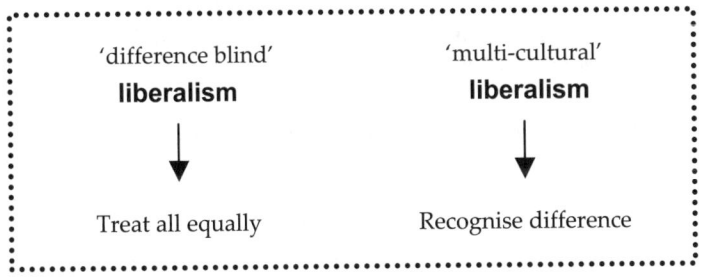

The tensions between these two forms of liberalism, reflective of the two strands of Australian nationalism, are evident. Difference-blind liberalism rejects multicultural liberalism because it appears to violate the principle of non-discrimination. Multicultural liberalism is critical of difference-blind liberalism because of the way that it desires and perpetuates homogeneity; its difference-blind principles reflect one set of values and one culture and alienates those who do not share them.

Both forms of liberalism have inherent flaws that will impede the exercise of personal liberty. Difference-blind liberalism needs to be rejected because of the way that it embraces the homogenous state. A

---

51 M Minow, 1990, *Making all the Difference: inclusion, exclusion and American Law*, Cornell University Press, pp 415-16.

difference-blind approach to equal access to education and treatment before the law ignores differences in experience which impede and constrain those from cultural backgrounds that differ from the dominant culture. In the context of this discussion, human rights violations – genocide, cultural genocide, racial discrimination – have occurred while Indigenous communities have been either under the protection of the legal system or granted equal status as citizens with other Australians. It appears that much of the racial conflict that exists in Australia is a result of the historical application of a model of assimilation cloaked in the rhetoric of difference-blind liberalism. It asserts that there is 'one law for all Australians' and embraces the myth of an egalitarian Australia. Formal equality does not work while inherent discrimination and cultural conflict within existing institutions are not addressed. Nor does it work while the focus is on equality of opportunity and fairness of processes rather than on equality of outcome.

However, the quest for substantive equality rather than formal equality, that is, measuring equality by results and impacts rather than the formal application of the same rules, will go some way towards recognising and countering the inherent bias in institutional forms.

Multicultural liberalism demands an understanding of the importance of the way that society creates spaces for different cultural groups. Multicultural liberalism recognises that different cultural values enrich society and allows cultures a space to develop and grow, promoting diversity. Members of such societies have more perspectives open to them from which they can learn and develop their authentic self. Criticism levelled at multicultural arrangements often relates to accusations of increased tensions created by allowing those differences to perpetuate. Another, more significant, problem arises when the emphasis on diversity acknowledges the group rather than the individual as the rights-holding entity. It is sometimes asserted that by vesting rights that are by nature communal in the group rather than the individual, those rights will be more effectively protected and enjoyed. This is especially so in relation to rights which relate to cultural identity, such as the right to speak a traditional language. Individual liberty is threatened and constrained by the demands of conforming to the practices and ideals of the group. A multiculturalism directed towards recognising groups at the expense of individual members not only fails to protect personal liberty but also will constrain the group, keeping it static rather than dynamic.

Group rights also assume that equality and tolerance occur within the group. When it does not, the individual may be left without redress.

The challenge remains. How should institutions recognise the relationship between the individual and the group? How should the state and legal system deal with difference? An alternative lies between the need to recognise the importance of group attachments and cultural practices and the protection of the freedom of the individual. The tensions can be countered by recognising the importance of group affiliation but limiting that recognition so that it provides *only a context* in which to pursue personal liberty. This means a recognition of difference beyond the tokenism of multiculturalism.

This requires a fluid, two-pronged approach: the development of targeted services for specific needs *and* improved access to mainstream services. It requires the identification of the factors that exclude people (their Aboriginality, racial prejudice, poor and ineffective policies) and the countering of those exclusions, providing pockets for participation and inclusion as well as continually working to ensure access to mainstream services. Mechanisms for effective participation transcend the constraints of strictly defined groups and promote a broader and more complex notion of difference by allowing the individual to organise with group affiliations. But they do not confine the individual to those groups.

Difference-blind liberalism and multicultural liberalism may seem incompatible because of the inherent tension between them. The choice seems to be whether to ignore cultural difference by using a model of difference-blind liberalism (which can lead to tensions when cultural groups feel that they are being suppressed and their values ignored) or the model of multicultural liberalism (where cultural groups are allowed to exist but the accommodation of their difference leads to tension). But these options do not have to stand in an either/or relationship to one another.

The two principles of substantive equality and effective participation lead towards a different kind of liberalism, an outcome-based liberalism. These principles heighten the importance of individual liberty through substantive equality. They contextualise individual liberty in a group context by promoting group alliances and alliance forming where groups intersect.

These principles link to the notion of contextualised individuality. Substantive equality recognises the paramount importance of personal liberty; effective participation allows for expression of group affiliation. Substantive equality promotes the supremacy of individual rights but recognises personal liberty requires some flexibility. Effective participation would recognise the ability to organise along group affiliation where the individual has chosen to identify with and join.

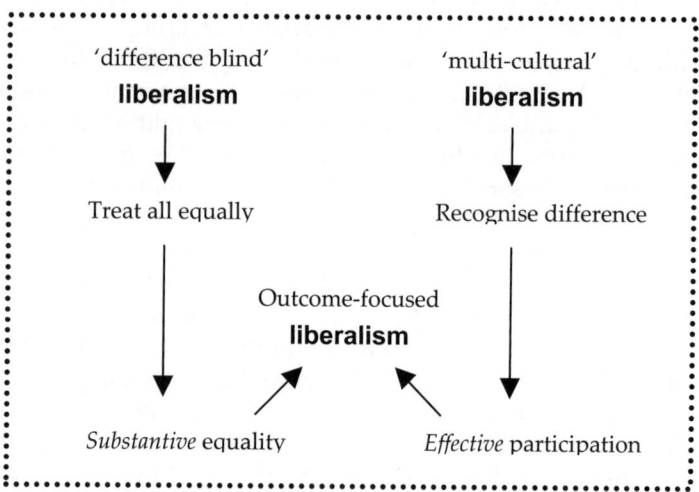

This form of outcome-based liberalism is faithful to the choices of the individual while recognising the importance and the benefits of diversity and difference. It seeks, by reliance on the principles of substantive equality and effective participation, to explore alternative institutional arrangements. It also seeks to promote individual choices whilst valuing difference and giving it an institutional form. In this way, the recognition of diversity and difference seeks to foster actual difference and incorporate it into institutional forms. It embraces John Dewey's idea that since institutions take on a life of their own and block new institutions from forming, they ideally need to be flexible and responsive. Dewey also reminded us that there was a need to constantly critique, review and revise what the state is doing; that this was a continuing process and democracy was a continuing project – an ongoing, experimental one.[52] These ideas have relevance for making Australian society more inclusive, equitable and democratic.

---

52 J Dewey, 1927, *The Public and Its Problems*, Ohio University Press. Dewey, like Mill, emphasised the importance of cultural membership for individual autonomy.

I will say more about these concepts when I discuss a program for institutional change in Chapter 5.

♦ ♦ ♦

If Australia is concerned with the protection of rights of Australians, Indigenous or otherwise, it needs to embrace these principles of substantive equality and effective participation. But it also needs to question how seemingly neutral laws perpetuate injustice. Australians must question the canonical status of their institutions. Understanding the way in which these institutions can compound racism is one way to begin looking more critically at them.

Those who are often treated as outsiders or even as threats to the dominant culture can actually deliver a great gift to the dominant culture; they can provide different values, different perspectives and therefore different starting points from which to consider concepts such as equality, fairness and democracy. They can also provide alternative starting points for institutional change. Indigenous people, as perennial outsiders, can offer Australians a different perspective on their institutions.

The appropriate and best starting point for protection of Indigenous rights is assessing what it is that Indigenous people want. There are two reasons for looking at the Indigenous agenda as the starting point for improving Indigenous rights.

- It is the embodiment of the principles of self-determination that people be able to make decisions about their lives. This allows for the achievement of real political self-determination, as it is finally seeking to provide Indigenous people with a political and legal framework that will represent their goals and vision.
- Indigenous people do not just highlight what it is that the Indigenous community needs; they offer alternative solutions, new starting points and new perspectives on institutional arrangements, highlighting weaknesses in institutions that many unquestioningly accept as being adequate and fair. Indigenous perspectives can facilitate changes that will create greater rights protection, not just for Indigenous people but for all Australians.

In the next chapter, I will look at the political and legal goals of the Indigenous community to get a sense of their parameters. I will then look at a framework for institutional change that could be a vehicle for achieving those improved rights protections.

Chapter 4
Indigenous aspirations: The starting point for rights protection

The following quote is taken from a 1992 Aboriginal Provisional Government (APG) paper entitled 'Intellectual Prisoners'.

> Whenever Aborigines are asked what it is they want in the long run, an extraordinary range of answers are given. To be equal, land rights, self-determination, to be Australian, sovereignty are among the many responses. Not all of these are, of course, inconsistent. But they do show a lack of common direction of thought among Aborigines. Until we agree on what we are aiming for, our energies will be unavoidably fractured, often heading all over the place. The quicker we agree about our destiny, the quicker we are likely to achieve.[1]

The idea of a developed dialogue on the content of Indigenous rights and aspirations *within* the Indigenous community is not new. What follows shares the view that there is an important dialogue that needs to take place and be developed within Indigenous communities about the scope and extent of specific political goals, needs and wants. There is a protocol and rhetoric within the politics of the Indigenous community that makes any consultation process complex and time-intensive. Despite the group solidarity that can be shown at a national level, Indigenous communities insist on having their own voice heard and this protocol needs to be observed and protected. Coupled with this is the consideration of how these agendas, particular to each community, come together at regional and national levels to ensure

---

1   Aboriginal Provisional Government, 1995, 'Intellectual prisoners', in I Moores (ed), *Voices of Aboriginal Australia: Past Present and Future*, Butterfly Books, p 319.

Indigenous people a stronger, more powerful political presence and voice.

What will be looked at here is what some of the answers, when those dialogues have taken place, *may* look like. As noted at the beginning of the book, this is not meant as a definitive or authoritative list. These political goals have been mapped by focusing on Indigenous notions of 'sovereignty' and 'self-determination'. The deconstruction of the political agenda of Indigenous people and their communities will begin with these key concepts, since these have been the two political aspirations that have been most centrally featured in the lexicon of Indigenous claims.

What 'Indigenous sovereignty' and 'Indigenous self-determination' might mean

Indigenous communities are diverse in culture and circumstance and therefore their needs are very different. Communities that are enclaves within urban areas, finding themselves a sub-group of a larger, non-Indigenous political unit, have different needs and strategies to those of Indigenous communities living in remote and distinct geographical areas where they may already be engaged in initiatives that can be categorised as decentralised self-governing actions. Aspirations will be specific to small communities – the need for a medical centre or a doctor, a school – but there is also a broader vision of the relationship that is sought with Australian society and its institutions that is expressed when needs are articulated.

Despite these cultural and geographical differences, there is much common ground in answer to the question 'What do you want?' The following conclusions seek to find the common ground that further and broader consultations within the Indigenous community may reveal.

Examples of Indigenous claims

This examination begins by looking at the contents of two documents that come from community-based claims for political action and justice: the Barunga statement and the Eva Valley statement.

The Barunga statement, presented in 1988 by Galarrwuy Yunupingu (Chairperson, Northern Land Council) and Wenten Rubuntja (Chairperson, Central Land Council) to then Prime Minister Bob Hawke, asserted these rights:

- self-determination and self-management;
- permanent control and enjoyment of ancestral lands;
- compensation for the loss of use of lands, there having been no extinction of original title;
- protection of and control of access to sacred sites, sacred objects, artefacts, designs, knowledge and works of art;
- the return of the remains of ancestors for burial in accordance with traditions;
- respect for promotion of Aboriginal identity, including the cultural, linguistic, religious and historical aspects, including the right to be educated in their own culture and history; and
- rights to life, liberty, security of person, food, clothing, housing, medical care, education and employment opportunities, necessary social services and other basic rights (in accordance with the Universal Declaration on Human Rights, the International Covenant on Economic, Social, and Cultural Rights, the International Covenant on Civil and Political Rights, and the Convention for the Elimination of all forms of Racial Discrimination).[2]

The Barunga statement also called on the federal government to pass laws to establish the following:

- a nationally elected Aboriginal and Islander organisation to oversee Aboriginal and Islander affairs;
- a national system of land rights; and
- a police and justice system that recognises customary laws and frees from discrimination any activity which may threaten identity or security, interfere with freedom of expression or association or otherwise prevent full enjoyment and exercise of universally recognised human rights and fundamental freedoms.[3]

To paraphrase, the Barunga statement focused on these issues.

- self-government and self-management;
- land and compensation for dispossession;
- protection of cultural heritage;
- recognition of customary law;

---

2   The Barunga statement, reproduced in I Moores (ed), 1995, *Voices of Aboriginal Australia: Past Present and Future*, Butterfly Books, p 332-33.
3   Ibid.

- protection of international human rights (as recognised under international law); and
- freedom from discrimination.

The claims to land and compensation for dispossession, protection of cultural heritage and recognition of customary law relate to rights that may be applied in a 'special' way to Indigenous people. The claims to the protection of international human rights (as recognised under international law) and the freedom from discrimination are sought to ensure that rights protections enjoyed by other Australians are extended to Indigenous people. This is a combination of claims for special treatment and equal rights, underlined by a strong demand for control of decision-making processes.

The Eva Valley statement lists the following aspirations:

We demand that:
- The Commonwealth honour its obligations under International Human Rights Instruments and International Law.
- The Commonwealth agrees to a negotiating process to achieve a lasting settlement with and for the benefit of all Aboriginal and Torres Strait Islander Peoples. Since time immemorial we have owned, occupied, used and enjoyed the continent and its islands in accordance with our Laws and Customs to the exclusion of the whole world. Since the arrival of non-Indigenous people our political and territorial integrity has been violated and that violation continues. This settlement process must recognise and address these historical truths. It must also redress the impact of our dispossession, marginalisation, destabilisation and disadvantage, including financial and material recompense.
- The Commonwealth take action in response to the High Court's decision on Native Title in accordance with the following principles:
  1. Recognition and protection of Aboriginal and Torres Strait Islander Rights
  2. The Commonwealth Government acknowledge that Aboriginal and Torres Strait Islander land title cannot be extinguished by grants of any interests.
  3. No grant of any interest on Aboriginal and Torres Strait Islander Title can be made without the informed consent of all the relevant title holders.
  4. Commonwealth Declaration of Aboriginal and Torres Strait Islander Title in reserves and other defined lands.
  5. Total security for Sacred Sites and Heritage Areas which provides for Aboriginal and Torres Strait Islander Peoples' absolute authority ...

To ensure that there is equity in and ownership of the negotiation process, it is essential that this body be provided with the resources to carry out the wishes of Aboriginal and Torres Strait Islander Peoples.[4]

As with the Barunga statement, there is a split emphasis on rights that may be identified as protecting 'Indigenous' rights – culture and heritage – and ensuring that *all* human rights are better protected. The Eva Valley statement was issued as a response to the debate around the *Native Title Act* 1993 (Cth) so it is predominantly concerned with land issues; however, its agenda reveals how those property interests are considered to be intimately connected with all other rights. The Eva Valley statement calls twice for the protection of human rights in general terms. Another aspect of note is that, like the Barunga statement, there is an emphasis on control and decision-making, on consultation, negotiation and consent. The Barunga statement includes expression of the need for recognition of 'historical truths', a recognition of past injustice.

The claims in those documents are reinforced by the rights asserted by Indigenous people and their leadership. I will take three examples, one each from Patrick Dodson, Geoff Clark and Galarrwuy Yunupingu.

In 1999, Patrick Dodson, first Chair of the Council for Aboriginal Reconciliation, delivered the 4th Vincent Lingiari Memorial Lecture, 'Until the Chains are Broken'. In his lecture, he identified some points that may be included in a treaty.

It may read something like this.

Equality: Aboriginal peoples have the right to all the common human rights and fundamental freedoms recognised in national and international law, as well as to our distinct rights as indigenous peoples.

Distinct characteristics and identities: Aboriginal peoples have the right to maintain and develop our distinct characteristics and identities, whilst taking part in the life of the country as a whole ...

Self-determination: Aboriginal peoples have the right to self determination. A right to negotiate our political status and to pursue economic, social and cultural development.

---

4   Eva Valley statement, reproduced in I Moores (ed), 1995, *Voices of Aboriginal Australia: Past Present and Future*, Butterfly Books, p 364.

INDIGENOUS ASPIRATIONS

Law: Aboriginal peoples have the right to our own law, customs and traditions, and equality before the National Law.

Culture: Aboriginal peoples have the right to our unique cultural traditions and customs. This includes aspects of our cultures such as designs, ceremonies, performances and technologies. We have the right to own and control our cultural and intellectual property, including our sciences, technologies, medicines, knowledge of flora and fauna, arts and performances. Our cultural property taken without consent shall be returned to us.

Spiritual and Religious Traditions: Aboriginal peoples have the right to our spiritual and religious traditions. This includes the right to preserve and protect our sacred sites, ceremonial objects and the remains of our ancestors.

Language: Aboriginal peoples have the right to our languages, histories, stories, oral traditions and names for people and places. This includes the right to be heard and to receive information in our own languages. In courts, other proceedings and in the criminal justice system, we shall have the right to understand and be understood, through interpreters and other appropriate ways.

Participation and partnerships: Aboriginal peoples have the right to participate in law and policy-making and in decisions that affect us. This includes the right to choose our own representatives. Governments shall obtain our consent before adopting these laws and policies. Governments shall negotiate partnerships with Aboriginal peoples' representative bodies at local, regional, State and National levels.

Economic and social development: Aboriginal peoples have the right to determine priorities and strategies for economic and social development. This includes the right to determine health, housing, and infrastructure, and other economic and social programs and, to the extent possible, to deliver these through our own organisations. There shall be recognition of the importance of empowerment for decision-making and development at regional and community levels. There shall be indigenous participation in all regional planning processes. Aboriginal peoples shall have full access to, and equitable outcomes from, participation in relevant mainstream programmes.

Special measures: Aboriginal peoples have the right to special measures to improve our economic and social conditions. This includes the areas of employment, education and training, housing and infrastructure, and health.

Education and training: Aboriginal peoples have the right to all forms and levels of public education and training. We also have the right to our own schools and to provide education in our own languages ...

Land and resources: Aboriginal peoples have the right to own and control the use of our land, waters and other resources. This includes the right to return of land and resources taken without our consent. Where this is not possible, we shall receive just compensation. Governments shall obtain our consent before giving approval to activities affecting our land and resources, including the development of mineral resources. We shall receive just compensation for any such activities.

Self-government: As a form of self-determination Aboriginal peoples have the right to self-government and autonomy in relation to our own affairs. This includes the right to determine the structure and membership of our self-governing institutions. Governments shall facilitate the negotiation of self-government and regional agreements.

Constitutional recognition: The Federal Parliament shall initiate processes leading to concrete constitutional change to recognise and protect the special place and rights of the Aboriginal peoples in the Australian polity.

Treaties and agreements: The Federal Parliament shall enact legislation establishing a framework for the negotiation of agreements with the Aboriginal peoples. Governments shall respect treaties and agreements entered into with Aboriginal peoples.

Ongoing processes: The Federal Parliament shall establish a discussion, research, information and negotiation forum to promote public awareness and to draft national legislation enacting principles of recognition, guidelines for public policy, and the framework for negotiation of agreements referred to above.[5]

There is the same balancing of 'special protection' and 'equal protection' running throughout Dodson's document that also stresses the need for control and consent, and involvement in decision-making processes. He identifies points of concern similar to those noted in the Barunga and the Eva Valley statements:

- land and compensation;
- customary law;
- cultural heritage (language, traditions, knowledge); and
- self-determination and self-government.

---

5   P Dodson, 2000, 'Until the Chains are Broken', 4th Vincent Lingiari Memorial Lecture, in M Grattan (ed), *Essays on Reconciliation*, Black Inc, p 264.

Dodson also includes these elements.

- education;
- economic development and the creation of an economic base;
- the importance of constitutional protection; and
- the development of a treaty and regional agreements.

Dodson broadens the claims examined in the Barunga and the Eva Valley statements, looking more holistically at rights protections. It is also important to remember that he is fresh from the experience of seeing the recognition of native title eroded by the legislature.

In setting out what should be included in a document for reconciliation, Geoff Clark, Chair of the Aboriginal and Torres Strait Islander Commission, suggests the following. It should:

- address the structural relationship between the Indigenous people and the Australian state;
- address the concerns of the Stolen Generations, including a formal apology and a process of compensation;
- include reference to Indigenous customary law; and
- provide an independent economic base for Indigenous people that removes the reliance on annual appropriations from parliaments.[6]

Like Dodson, Clark stresses the importance of an economic base and the need to address the 'structural relationship' through a treaty and regional agreements. Like the drafters of the Eva Valley statement, he emphasises the need to recognise past injustices (such as the Stolen Generations) and, in consensus with the previous examples, the need for the recognition of customary law.

Galarrwuy Yunupingu made the following suggestions as to what a treaty should include:

> Recognition of land rights is the key to Aboriginal self-determination. It is the basis for our development of a secure social, cultural and economic base. It gives us the basis for claiming compensation and achieving proper health, education, legal and child care services. The constitution must restore our rights to land under secure title, guarantee our access to lands and sites of Aboriginal significance on land which cannot be restored to us, give us full control of our own lands and compensate us for our lands which

---

6 G Clark, 2000b, 'Not Much Progress', in M Grattan (ed), *Reconciliation*, Black Ink, p 233.

have been alienated ... The Constitution should also guarantee the preservation of our social and cultural heritage and compensate us for the way in which they have been eroded at the hands of invaders. It should provide for Aboriginal people to develop a secure economic base. It must be the beginning of true self-determination for us.[7]

These claims contain the same holistic aspirations identified by Dodson and Clark:

- self-determination;
- land rights and compensation;
- an economic base;
- Constitutional recognition; and
- cultural heritage.

Yunupingu's statement was made two years before the Barunga statement was presented to the federal government. His comments reflect the currents running through the Indigenous rights agenda even when particular issues – land, the Stolen Generations – may come to the fore and seem to eclipse others. Highlighting as he does the common threads woven into the Indigenous rights agenda over a 15-year period, he shows how little has been achieved in relation to rights protection, disadvantage and unsettled issues.

The 'S' word

Dialogue about rights protection between Indigenous and non-Indigenous Australians is stilted with open dialogue confined by lack of forum, ignorance by non-Indigenous Australians of the issues and distrust on both sides. Given the enormous impact intrusive government policies have had on the lives of Indigenous people, it is not surprising that there is suspicion of any initiatives to improve the relationship between Indigenous and non-Indigenous Australians. This has meant that efforts to reconcile the Indigenous population with the rest of Australian society have often been clumsy, misdirected and largely unsuccessful.

One obstacle in the debate has been the confusion that surrounds the use of the word 'sovereignty'. It is a term that has become a

---

7   G Yunupingu, 1987, 'What the Aboriginal people want', *The Age*, 26 August; and in B Attwood and A Markus (eds), 1999, *The Struggle for Aboriginal Rights: A Documentary History*, Allen & Unwin, p 314.

catch-phrase for Indigenous people in expressing their vision for the future but a phrase that is met with confusion and suspicion from non-Indigenous people who understand the word only in its context under international law. They see the claim as radical, subversive and dangerous and they therefore strongly oppose it.

The notion of Indigenous people as a sovereign people derives from the fact that Indigenous people have never ceded their land and continue to feel separate, both in identity and in the way they are treated differently from other Australians.

Consider the basis for a treaty as explained by Galarrwuy Yunupingu.

> A treaty which is recognised by international convention must state that:
> - Aboriginal people are the indigenous sovereign owners of Australia and adjacent islands since before 1770 and as such have rights and treaty rights,
> - their sovereignty was never ceded, and
> - the doctrine of *terra nullius* cannot be supported in international law as the legal basis for European occupation of, and acquisition of sovereignty over, our land.[8]

This reminds me of something my father wrote.

> It is an historical fact that from the very inception of British colonisation, the indigenous people of this country have been treated as a separate society. However, when we project this fact in our aim of achieving sovereignty and of our struggle for compensation for dispossession and for economic independence that will allow us to run our own affairs, people say 'You can't do that – it's divisive'.[9]

What both men are emphasising is the alienation and disempowerment that many feel:

- We do not fit into this society; they do not want us.
- They do not accept us.
- They do not want our values.
- We want to do things our way.

---

8 Ibid.
9 P Behrendt, 1995, 'Aboriginal Sovereignty: Australian Republic: A Catalogue of Questions and Answers', in I Moores (ed), *The Voices of Aboriginal Australia: Past, Present, Future*, Butterfly Books, p 399.

The word 'sovereignty' within the lexicon of Indigenous rights discourse has been attached to various political visions to gain the ability to live life as Indigenous people choose, to exercise decision-making processes.

I want to argue that the notion of sovereignty goes to the heart of the restructuring of the relationship between Indigenous and non-Indigenous Australia and that the 'recognition of sovereignty' is linked to the recognition of the uniqueness of individual identity and history. To understand what sovereignty might mean, it is useful to begin by looking at what have been considered by non-Indigenous Australians to have been the most radical explanations of the term.

Very few activists have claimed that sovereignty embraces notions of statehood and succession, instead advocating that the appropriate way to ensure the effective protection of Indigenous rights and self-determination is though separatism. Others have put forward the notion of sovereignty as an option, stating quite clearly that it is but one option open to the Indigenous people to take, believing that for true political self-determination to take place, Indigenous people need to know what all their options are.

Kevin Gilbert, the Aboriginal poet, artist and activist, was one of the strongest and most passionate advocates of sovereignty. In a draft treaty written in consultation with Aboriginal Members of the Sovereign Aboriginal Coalition at Alice Springs in 1987, Gilbert wrote the following points about a 'Sovereign Position':

> 1.1.3 Our Sovereign Aboriginal Ownership, Possession and Sovereign Root Title to these our Land and our People have never been lost, removed or ceded in any form or manner by any *legal* act or claim ...
>
> 1.1.5 We are free to manage our own affairs both internally and externally to the fullest possible extent, in the proper exercise of our Sovereign Right as a Nation ...
>
> 1.1.7 Our Sovereign Aboriginal Nation, fulfilling the criteria of Statehood, having Inherent Possessory Root Title to Lands, a permanent population and a representative governing body according to our indigenous traditions, having the ability to enter relations with other States, possesses the right to autonomy in self-determination of our political status, to freely pursue our economic, social and cultural development and to retain our rights in religious matters, tradition and traditional practice.

1.1.8 We, the Sovereign Aboriginal People are to be accorded our right and proper recognition as a People and a Nation State, subjects of international law.[10]

Gilbert and his co-authors envisaged a single Indigenous nation with the same status as other nations.

The claim to sovereignty has also been a central platform of the APG who have long been strong advocates of talking about what sovereignty should mean and highlighting that there has always been strong community support for this dialogue. In the July 1992 APG papers, the following proposal for what the exercise of sovereignty would mean was set out.:

> *Let it be clearly understood*: the Aboriginal Provisional Government wants an Aboriginal state to be established, with all of the essential control being vested back into Aboriginal communities ... There will *not* be a need for all Aboriginal people to live on Aboriginal land. Some may choose to do so, and some may choose to continue to live under the jurisdiction of white Australia ... Nor would Aboriginal people have to live in a particular small area on Aboriginal lands. The areas would be scattered far and wide around Australia and would be the land needed by local Aboriginal communities ... [E]ach Aboriginal community would determine its own form of legal system appropriate to its community situation ... There would be no point in transferring white power to an Aboriginal Provisional Government which simply imposed the same policies from above. The local communities must have absolute control over their day-to-day activities and the direction in which the local Aboriginal communities are to move. The residual powers of negotiating with foreign governments for trade, coordination of some uniformity between Aboriginal communities and so on, would be vested in the Aboriginal Provisional Government. Election to the APG would be via the local community controlled councils ... The Aboriginal Government would operate alongside all other government, and not be subordinate to it ... In exchange for Aboriginal people giving up to perhaps half of the country to white Australians, there would need to be some compensation package.[11]

This statement calls for a 'state', but not in the sense of a separate country. There is no concept of compelling Indigenous people to live in a particular area. There is, however, a clear claim to jurisdiction at a

---

10 Reproduced in Attwood and Markus, 1999, pp 312-13.
11 Aboriginal Provisional Government, 'Towards Aboriginal sovereignty', reproduced in Attwood and Markus, 1999, p 327.

community level, particularly for the 'day-to-day' activities. The APG model proposed in this paper does envisage Indigenous representation at the national level that would take responsibility for the coordination between communities (national issues) and for negotiations with other governments. It is this last power – the ability to deal with governments – that takes the proposal closest to including elements that would be seen as a form of sovereignty as it would be understood under international law.

I want to now consider the way that other Indigenous people have used the concept of sovereignty to give a sense of how the term is used at a grass-roots community level.

Lisa Bellear, author, artist and social worker, shows that sovereignty clearly has a meaning for her in the way she uses it. She uses the word in a way that shows its conception goes to the heart of her political vision:

> Sovereignty is essential and you can't get away from it. They talked about the treaty back in 1988, but the lawyers knew that if you have a treaty you have to talk about sovereignty and land rights and look at compensation and reparation. We have to have a say. Indigenous people have to be treated with more respect ... We have to figure out what sovereignty means.[12]

The concepts that Ms Bellear talks about are those of respect for cultural difference and the participation in democratic processes. Her statement is reflective of the feelings of many Indigenous people living in the urban community. Her vision seeks a transference of power, a restructuring of the relationship between Indigenous and non-Indigenous Australians. Ms Bellear acknowledges that the meaning, content and implications of sovereignty are discussions that Indigenous Australians still have to undertake within our communities.

Kerry Reed-Gilbert, activist and writer, describes with great passion the way in which the refusal to sign a treaty and the continual attempts, overt and subversive, by Indigenous people to resist the institutions of the dominant culture combine to show that the sovereignty of Indigenous Australians that existed in 1788 has not been eroded:

> Sovereignty is us as a people being the prior owners of this country and never losing our sovereign rights as that people. Our own self-determination as black people has been going on 205 years after invasion. When Cook landed here as the first boat people he tried to

---

12   L Bellear, interview with author, 27 August 1997.

take our sovereign rights as the peoples of this country. But he never did. We have never lost our sovereign rights. And we've never lost our own need for self-determination … When you talk about self-determination and sovereignty, you are talking about our human rights, our rights as the owners of this land. Our sovereignty needs to be recognised. When it becomes recognised, people will start acknowledging that we have had, in our own way, self-determination for 205 years … When you see sovereignty, self-determination, equal rights, human rights, they are all empowered into that one thing. I see them as our basic needs. As the needs we have been fighting for.[13]

Human rights, basic needs, decision-making processes, recognition of past injustice, sovereignty and self-determination all weave into Ms Reed-Gilbert's vision of sovereignty. Importantly, she believes that the recognition of sovereignty is a device by which other rights can be achieved. Rather than being the *aim* of political advocacy, it is a *starting point* for recognition of rights and inclusion in democratic processes. It is seen as a footing, a recognition, from which to demand those rights and transference of power from the Australian state, not a footing from which to separate from it.

Similarly, Mark McMillan, Senior Researcher at Ngiya, the Australian Institute of Law, Policy and Practice, clearly conceptualises the recognition of sovereignty as a crucial starting point for the achievement of rights. He sees recognition of sovereignty as a necessary building block to creating a political environment that will move away from the paternalism of past government policies and allow for the creation of new institutions. It is clear that he is seeking a transformation of the relationship with Australian society and increased autonomy for Indigenous people.

> If there is to be a new relationship between Indigenous and non-Indigenous Australians that is premised on mutual respect, then recognition of sovereignty must be the cornerstone of this productive relationship. If there is not this level of recognition, Indigenous Australians will forever be caught within the colonial construct. The law and the 'psychological *terra nullius*' that you talk about is completely at odds with the factual reality. This factual reality (which every Australian recognises) is that Indigenous Australians were here long before contact. When this factual reality is realised in this new relationship, sovereignty must be the logical premise that underpins it. Once there is this acknowledgement of sovereignty,

---

13 K-R Gilbert, interview with author, 22 January 2003.

I do not think that it will be a far stretch for all to embrace the ideas and ideals of Indigenous self-determination. Included in these conceptions of self-determination is a comprehensive rights framework that protects the rights tied to this recognition of sovereignty.[14]

Self-determination and sovereignty are interlinked for Mark McMillan. The recognition of sovereignty is conceptualised again as a step that has to take place to provide a strong foundation for the exercise of self-determination.

Sovereignty is also seen as something that can be exercised by Indigenous people. This aspect of sovereignty is reinforced by the National Aboriginal Island Health Organisation (NAIHO):

> Sovereignty is not a vague legal concept. Sovereignty is a practical and achievable goal and, for Aboriginal people, can be defined as recognition of our Aboriginal rights. Sovereignty can be demonstrated as Aboriginal people controlling all aspects of their lives and destiny. Sovereignty is independent action. It is Aborigines doing things as Aboriginal people, controlling those aspects of our existence which are Aboriginal. *These include our culture, our economy, our social lives and our indigenous political institutions.* Wrapped up in all of this is health, housing, education, legal matters and land rights, and many other things ... [when] Aboriginal people are able to exercise absolute control over these essential areas without penalty being imposed by non-Aboriginal society, then our Aboriginal sovereignty will be recognised ...
>
> *This is not apartheid or separatism*; we are not saying send all the blacks to the territory and let them run it and have nothing to do with the rest of Australia ... Aboriginal sovereignty can be recognised and actioned without destroying the Commonwealth; it may be hard but it is possible ... Aboriginal people can exist as sovereign, identified, indigenous nations *within* the Commonwealth of Australia.[15]

Sovereignty in this sense becomes a pragmatic goal because it seeks to change the structural relationship between Indigenous and non-Indigenous Australians even when it is linked to the recognition and enjoyment of other human rights. The NAIHO views sovereignty as decentralised, grass-roots concept. It is about exercising autonomy,

---

14 M McMillan, interview with author, 18 January 2003.
15 National Aboriginal Island Health Organisation (NAIHO), 1985, Written comment, NAIHO Conference, <www.kooriweb.org/foley/news/story8.html>, accessed 19 December 2002.

both at an individual level and as a 'people'. This pragmatic view believes that Indigenous people can assert sovereignty in their day-to-day actions, that there is a personal aspect to sovereignty.

The writer and activist Roberta Sykes talks about the recognition of sovereignty on a personal level. She relates sovereignty to her daily existence, using the term to describe the way that she seeks autonomy from the state and control over the decisions in her life. What she resists is the interference of government into the affairs of the Indigenous community:

> While I don't think we can force the white people to acknowledge self-determination and the sovereignty of Aboriginal people for quite a long time, there is absolutely no reason why we shouldn't work on it and develop it in ourselves and in our own community until it is concrete there so that it can no longer be ignored. I see myself and the things I am involved in as building up that thought that we inside our own community determine what we are going to do and go out and do it, not just as an individual but as a group by assisting each other in whatever way we can actually do things and know you are doing it on behalf of our people.[16]

She elaborates in the context of education:

> When you have other things like governments sending people away on scholarships, that doesn't add to our self-determination, it detracts from it because the government can say who will go and what they can do. And they can do that through their funding. The impetus for going may come from the community but the choice of which area and how and when is all determined by the availability of government funding. It is not self-determination.[17]

Sykes is referring to the freedom of the individual to live the way he or she wants to live, an authentic self. While being conscious of, even defined by, the cultural group she identifies with, she does not feel confined by the politics of the group. Sykes has been an active advocate of Indigenous rights and her perspective reveals that the lack of interest in discussions of Indigenous sovereignty by the government has not dampened the enthusiasm of Indigenous people in exploring the concept.

Through language that is as moral as it is political and legal, Indigenous people are attaching a unique interpretation to the term

---

16 R Sykes, interview with author, 20 December 1997.
17 Ibid.

sovereignty. It includes concepts such as representative government and democracy, the recognition of cultural distinctiveness and notions of the freedom of the individual that are embodied in liberalism. These claims take place by seeking a new relationship with the Australian state with increased self-government and autonomy, though not the creation of a new country.

Sovereignty, not statehood

What is most striking is the use of the word sovereignty amongst Indigenous people who have adopted the term devoid of its implications under international law, showing primarily the organic development of the term in a domestic political context. In this popular appropriation of the word, political aspirations to the recognition of sovereignty include an aspiration to greater community autonomy but this falls short of advocating a separation from the Australian state. The notion captures the essence of *both* a separate cultural entity and historical dispossession *and* the exclusion and lack of consent involved in the creation of the modern Australian state. It is acknowledged by members of the Indigenous community that their communities do not have the resources, infrastructure or desire to be separated from the Australian state. Instead, they need to be empowered to build that independence within pockets of Australia.

As Getano Lui, former Chair of the Torres Strait Regional Authority, has said of the Torres Strait Islands:

> [o]ur long-term aim is to become independent of ATSIC but, at the same time, to work in conjunction with ATSIC. We are not attempting to break away from our brothers and sisters on the mainland nor do we want to break away from Australia.[18]

By deciphering the content of the strongest claims of political self-determination, it is clear that there is more common ground and possibility for accommodating the agenda of Indigenous populations than has been previously acknowledged or explored and that fear of destabilisation by the recognition of Indigenous sovereignty is misplaced. When all this is considered, we come fairly close to the formulation of what sovereignty might mean to the APG. They had

---

18 G Lui, 1994, 'Self-Government in the Torres Strait Islands', in C Fletcher (ed), *Aboriginal Self-Determination in Australia*, Australian Institute of Aboriginal and Torres Strait Islander Studies, p 127.

advocated for autonomous self-governance with a focus on local communities, exercise of jurisdiction and greater autonomy, an economic base, a reformulation of the relationship between Indigenous and non-Indigenous people and a structural change. Their vision begins to looks much less peripheral, radical or unachievable than it once might have seemed.

The recognition of Indigenous sovereignty is not a threat to the sovereignty of the Australian state but it does question the legitimacy of that authority, accuses it of historically excluding Indigenous people and of continuing with that exclusion today. It seeks a fundamentally different relationship, one that will change through a range of initiatives that, in totality, can be characterised as self-determination.

The use of the term sovereignty in Indigenous rights advocacy illustrates how a technical legal term can leak into the political rhetoric of a disadvantaged and alienated group, become a catch-phrase for political goals and transform into a word with a different meaning. In this way, language can actually confine a debate in the absence of a clear understanding by both parties as to what is meant by the lexicon of political terms being used. This highlights how a semantic block can occur when two sides in a debate have different understandings of the vocabulary they are using, a stand-off that has, and continues to, stifle debate about Indigenous aspirations and rights.

It may seem to non-Indigenous Australians that the use of the word 'sovereignty' has been used in a misleading way. It has been difficult to find another catchword, expression or phrase within the English language which could state more accurately the claims of the Indigenous community. The semantic confusion reflects the poverty of political and institutional language, the limited number of institutional alternatives available and the uniqueness of the relationship that Aboriginal people seek to forge with Australian society.

Compounding the confusion is the use of the term 'self-determination', often used in the same sentence as sovereignty.

In the *First Report 1993* of the Aboriginal and Torres Strait Islander Social Justice Commissioner (1993 ATSISJC report) self-determination is spoken about in the following terms:

> Self-determination is intimately related to calls for a treaty and constitutional recognition of indigenous rights. They all flow from an endeavour to regain recognition of our original rights to the freedom and control of our lives which were lost with the invasion of our lands and to gain a recognition of those rights which is secure. On a basis which is not dependant on grace or favour or welfare but in

recognition of our original place and our continuing distinct cultural identity which we wish to retain.[19]

The absence of self-determination is experienced by Aboriginal and Torres Strait Islander people in an intimate, daily way. Confinement to mainstream government services relating to health, housing, education and employment is, to many indigenous peoples, reminiscent of the missionary days.[20]

The exercise of self-determination by Aboriginal and Torres Strait Islander communities most frequently centres on the provision of community services. The aim is not merely to participate in the delivery of those services, but to penetrate their design and inform them with indigenous cultural values. The result is not merely services which are better structured to reflect the needs and identity of particular communities: there can be a resultant improvement in the effectiveness and efficiency of these services. The assumption of indigenous control has the potential to create benefits which flow to the Aboriginal and Torres Strait Islander community. It can also bring benefit to the wider community.[21]

Recognition in the Constitution and through a treaty, exercise of autonomy, control over the delivery of services and the attainment of freedom to live life the way one wants – these seem to be key concepts that describe the results of the recognition of sovereignty described above and embrace the claims and assertions canvassed at the beginning of the chapter.

Sovereignty and self-determination

The recognition of sovereignty and exercise of self-determination seem to lead to claims for the same rights. Some people have stated that the recognition of sovereignty is the historical and cultural base from which to build self-determination for Indigenous people. This way of imagining the relationship between the two concepts embraces sovereignty as a concept that belongs to Indigenous people while seeking to utilise the use of the tools of self-determination identified in the 1993 ATSISJC report. Others have adopted the term self-determination without reference to the notion of sovereignty, perhaps understanding that the tools used for self-determination will lead to

---

19   ATSISJC, 1993, p 50.
20   ATSISJC, 1993, p 56.
21   ATSISJC, 1993, p 56.

the socio-economic improvement and increased autonomy that are linked to the notion of sovereignty.

There are several points to note about the political use of these terms that go some way towards explaining why confusion between the two terms has emerged.

- The then Federal Minister for Aboriginal Affairs, Gerry Hand, used the term self-determination in 1987 as part of the government's policy on Indigenous issues. In principle, the idea was to allow Indigenous people to contribute to government policy formulation through ATSIC, establishing a bureaucracy guided by representative members of the Indigenous community. In this context, self-determination became a simile for self-management, creating Indigenous bureaucrats working within the government system. It was not a policy designed to create self-determination in the sense that the word has been interpreted by Indigenous people or as it is defined under international law. In light of this, there was some reluctance to use the term for fear it would imply approval of the federal government's agenda. The term sovereignty became much more popular as it expressed a broader, more relevant vision. Consider the way that Geoff Scott, Deputy CEO of ATSIC, talks about the difference between self-determination, which has been used as a slogan by the government, and sovereignty, to which he attaches an political and legal interpretation.

> We must be frank and open about the past efforts of government and our responses if we are to progress at all. The government embarked on a policy of 'self-determination', but what was offered was a policy of self-management in the guise of 'self-determination'. What surfaced was a continuation of the assimilationist policy of previous regimes ... The result was the government 'allowing' good little blackfellas to manage themselves if they were compliant and quiet ... Our advocates who used this word 'self-determination' in its true sense and espoused the necessity of the recognition of Aboriginal sovereignty were belittled and excluded from the operational context and actual debate in the Indigenous affairs arena ... Sovereignty is not something a government can 'give'; it is already possessed by the people.[22]

---

22 G Scott, interview with author, 7 January 2003.

- The term self-determination has come to the fore again in the lexicon of Indigenous rights as there has been increased activity within the UN. Indigenous peoples have sought to bring pressure on the Australian government to ensure that rights recognised under international law and international human rights instruments are protected. This has included utilising the UN reporting system under the International Covenant on Civil and Political Rights (ICCPR), the International Covenant on Economic, Social and Cultural Rights (ICESCR) and CERD. This international focus has also increased due to participation in the Working Group on Indigenous Peoples and the development of the Draft Declaration on the Rights of Indigenous Peoples. These activities in the international arena have facilitated a return to the use of self-determination as a term encompassing Indigenous aspirations.
- There are also pragmatic and strategic reasons why there has been a return to the language of the term self-determination in recent years. For advocates who understand that the recognition of sovereignty and self-determination lead to the embrace of the same issues and political aims, there is a strategic response that sees the advantages of using the term self-determination instead of the more political contentious term of sovereignty. The adoption of the term self-determination avoids the hysteria and suspicion that surrounds the word sovereignty in the non-Indigenous community.

Deciphering the content of Indigenous sovereignty and self-determination

Sovereignty and self-determination lead to or embody a list of claims or a series of tools. The following is an attempt to pull out some of the obvious and recurring threads tied together in the notions of the recognition of sovereignty and the exercise of self-determination.

The recognition of past injustices

Indigenous peoples demand recognition of past injustices, including the failure to recognise Indigenous sovereignty and laws, dispossession and government policies, particularly the policy of removing Indigenous children. This recognition of past injustices also includes a claim for the recognition of prior sovereignty and prior ownership.

This form of acknowledgment is not just about recognising past injustices; it is about recognising the colonial legacy that Indigenous people live with today, of the links between past and present. Such acknowledgment shows respect for Indigenous people and their experiences and it acknowledges that the impact of colonisation is experienced every day by Indigenous people. It is also about getting a respect Indigenous people have yet to receive from the dominant culture. It seeks to counter the exclusion of Indigenous perspectives from Australian folklore, an exclusion which has led to an Australian national identity that remains silent on those experiences and adds to feelings of alienation felt by Indigenous people.

Recognising the truth of Australia's past seems a small step towards dramatically changing race relations in Australia but it is an essential first step to creating a political environment that is more inclusive and therefore more protective of Indigenous rights. Linda Burney, former Director-General of the NSW Department of Aboriginal Affairs, notes the connection between public perception and rights:

> It seems to me that citizenship in the civic sense must be about participation in the life of the community, as a full member of that society. That means citizenship has to be about belonging. There needs to be both knowledge and awareness of the political and social systems involved and there needs to be a level of shared faith in those systems ... I want to suggest that the real reason why Australian identity has always been such a problem for other Australians is simply because the Aboriginal element has been left out.[23]

Recognition of past injustices is crucial to the creation of a new relationship between Indigenous and non-Indigenous Australians. Patrick Dodson sees recognition of our history as a key pre-requisite in any form of reconciliation:

> Reconciliation can mean different things. But, above all, it must involve some form of agreement that deals with legacies of our history, and takes us forward as a nation. It means achieving practical and demonstrable outcomes through recognising indigenous cultures and achievements and through improving the lives and circumstances of indigenous people... My grandfather taught me that the river is the river and the sea is the sea. Each has its own

---

23   L Burney, 2000, 'Not Just a Challenge, an Opportunity', in M Grattan (ed), *Reconciliation*, Black Ink, pp 70-1.

complex patterns, origins and stories, and even though they come together, they will always exist in their own right. Non-indigenous Australians cannot be expected to learn or understand the lessons of my grandfather, but simply to respect that they are central to my identity. This acceptance of diversity is another important element of reconciliation.[24]

This overturning of Australia's psychological *terra nullius* is linked to symbolic nation-building, to a change in the structural relationship. Paul Behrendt speaks of this nation-building in a way that includes the idea of legitimacy:

> The Aboriginal people of this continent have the inalienable right to their own sovereignty, no matter what political system is in place. Without the recognition of Aboriginal sovereignty, no government, republic and monarchy had any legitimacy in this country. Legitimacy is the most valuable gift that Aboriginal people can give a republic, and that can only happen with the recognition by other Australians that the Aboriginal People and the sovereign people of this land.[25]

This step towards legitimacy is also an indicator of good faith and *bona fides*. Tony Birch, historian and poet, reveals that acknowledgment of injustice is important to repairing the relationship between Indigenous peoples and other Australians:

> I would like to see the government say: 'We're serious about self-determination and sovereignty and to show that we're serious we are going to recognise land rights in law. We don't need a treaty to recognise that we invaded a land which was occupied. We don't need a treaty to give you back your land and to compensate your families for having their children abducted.' I would say to them: do that first and then maybe we can act in good faith. I couldn't imagine any Aboriginal person sitting at a table and signing a document with a non-Aboriginal government, at the moment, and see it as having any realistic basis, no matter what it says. Even where they have treaties, like the Treaty of Waitangi, Maori people have suffered a lot since 1840 when I think that treaty was signed. I would rather see something happen first before I saw any signing of documents.[26]

---

24 P Dodson, 1996, 'Reconciliation Misunderstood', *The Australian*, 13 September, p 12.
25 P Behrendt, 1995, p 398.
26 T Birch, interview with author, 23 January 2003.

Autonomy and decision-making powers

Much of the aspiration to the recognition of sovereignty and the exercise of self-determination are related to a claim of control over decision-making that affects people's day-to-day lives. For example, Geoff Clark has said:

> Indigenous people are seeking the ability to exercise choice in our lives. So much of the history that has shaped this country had denied us any choice ... [W]e seek the opportunity to exercise choice. Indigenous people have always been told where to go, what to do, where we can socialise and with whom. We have been directed as to who we can marry and when and where we can practice our cultures and beliefs. We were told it was for our own good.[27]

Similarly, Jenny Munro, Chairperson of the Metropolitan Local Land Council in Sydney, states:

> until we have the control of our destiny and *we* decide as a group, as a nation, where our people and our destiny lies, we are not able to take those steps needed to assure our destiny is fulfilled. It will never happen while a white man tells us where to step, where to put our feet.[28]

Aboriginal activist Charles Perkins noted that the paternalism of the past in decision-making about Indigenous people needs to be broken:

> From an Aboriginal viewpoint, I believe that our mistake over the years has been to look towards the white people, in positions of influence, to solve our problems. This has been our fundamental error. Recent history tells us that we should have known for the past 200 years. It is amazing to me, that we, the Aboriginal people, have not yet absorbed that white people in responsible positions are no better than us (in fact they are worse, given their educational background), at managing or solving difficult individual or community problems.[29]

---

27 Clark, 2000b, pp 229, 231.
28 J Munro, 1995, 'Aboriginal Deaths in Custody Result from the Paternalistic Status Quo', in I Moores (ed), *Voices of Aboriginal Australia: Past, Present, Future*, Butterfly Books, p 215.
29 C Perkins, 1994, 'Self Determination and Managing the Future', in C Fletcher (ed), *Aboriginal Self-Determination in Australia*, Australian Institute of Aboriginal and Torres Strait Islander Studies, p 34.

Indigenous people seek autonomy from the state through decentralised forms of government and institutions. This claim to self-government can be seen as the seeking of mechanisms by which the members of the Indigenous community can live with greater control over the decision-making processes that control their lives. This calls (a) for the greater use of community-based self-government institutions and (b) a request for the decentralisation of the existing governmental institutions combines the seemingly conflicting aims of autonomy and inclusion.

Such decision-making power is demanded at a grass-roots level since it is at the local community level that people feel more empowered to initiate changes; this is where such change will have the greatest impact on their lives. Smaller units allow for more effective representative government, especially if there is delegation of decision-making to the local community level. This is especially so for geographically remote communities that may take control of issues such as the disciplining of juveniles who commit petty crime.[30] In such geographically distinct and remote areas there is larger scope for mechanisms of autonomy, such as the development of local councils with ordinance-making powers.[31]

---

30 Such programs were recommended by the RCIADIC and led to the establishment of several community-based programs that allowed the community to deal with problems, such as intoxicated persons who would have been arrested and placed in police holding cells but were allowed to stay in safe houses where they were looked after by members of the community. Similar programs have been designed to allow Indigenous communities to deal with problems of juvenile crime such as vandalism.

31 An example of the economic independence that is achievable for communities when they have a land base are the recent initiatives of the Jawoyn Association in Katherine. The group has been able to accumulate $5 million which is being used for 'economic, social, cultural, training and employment goals.' This asset base is the result of a tourist business and of negotiations with mining interests. ('Jawoyn launch five year plan', *ATSIC News*, April 1997, p 16). The Pitjantjantjara have been able to establish an area of land, claimed back through legislative provisions, on which they have introduced their own rules at a local government level. The area now held by the community covers a large, area of land in South Australia, towards the border with the Northern Territory. Courts have affirmed the right of the Pitjantjantjara to legislate at this level: *Gerhardy v Brown* (1985) 159 CLR 70.

However, the wish for greater autonomy and independence is also expressed by those living in geographically integrated urban communities. There the challenges are greater for institutions that can allow for decentralised decision-making that empowers the individual but it is at this level that Indigenous people most actively seek inclusion in democratic processes.

These expressions of self-determination are already taking place at a community level. The 1993 ATSISJC report stated:

> [a]t a broader level, many Aboriginal community councils and associations take on the essential functions of local government bodies. They perform a role effectively equivalent to the third tier within the hierarchy of government. While there are many complex issues concerning legal structures and funding arrangements which affect the ability of Aboriginal councils and associations to genuinely assume full determinative roles within their own communities, they not only have the potential to establish and deliver essential services: in the fullest form they can operate as the medium of full self-government.[32]

Marcia Langton, Foundation Chair of Indigenous Studies at Melbourne University, makes the same point about governance structures in Cape York:

> The view of Aboriginal owners of Cape York is that Aboriginal self-government has already existed and that this is not a new concept that we are discussing now. If we look at it from their point of view, we can see that Indigenous self-government in Australia is the longest surviving egalitarian system of government possibly in the world, one which balanced the rule of law with personal autonomy through a philosophy of respect for those who went before as well as for those who come after us. It is also recognised by the Aboriginal owners of Cape York that the disruption of historical colonialism and the new colonial strategies have altered or hemmed in Aboriginal ways of governing ... So when we speak of Aboriginal self-government in Cape York, although we are referring to it as a system of Aboriginal government, it is one which functions in outstations and in Aboriginal villages and settlements with limited resources.[33]

---

32   ATSISJC, 1993, p 59.
33   M Langton, 1994, 'Indigenous Self-Government and Self-Determination: Overlapping Jurisdiction at Cape York', in C Fletcher (ed), *Aboriginal Self-Determination in Australia*, Australian Institute of Aboriginal and Torres Strait Islander Studies, pp 131, 135.

This wish for independence and autonomy is intricately related to the wish to gain economic self-sufficiency, a way of release from the stranglehold of the welfare system. Paul Behrendt notes that this autonomy and these decision-making processes are dependant upon an economic independence: 'Aboriginal people are now saying that we wish to control our own affairs. We know better than anyone what our problems are and how they can best be addressed. We can only do that if we have economic independence.'[34]

Property rights and compensation

Also intricately linked to the notions of sovereignty and autonomy is the need for land and the recognition of property rights. This includes the recognition of prior ownership, an extension of the limited recognition of native title rights recognised under common law and the recognition of the need for land as an economic base for dispossessed communities.

In the draft treaty written in consultation with Aboriginal Members of the Sovereign Aboriginal Coalition in 1987, Kevin Gilbert demanded that the Commonwealth and States:

- recognise original ownership, possession and Root Title of Aboriginals to Land,
- restore immediately all unalienated 'Crown' lands, including State and National Parklands, Aboriginal reserves, travelling stock reserves,
- negotiate Aboriginal State Boundaries,
- recognise that Aboriginal State Lands are Sovereign Aboriginal Lands with title in perpetuity and inalienable,
- agree that the Aboriginal land base be not less than 40% of the total landmass of each 'Australian State' land holding,
- agree to the Aboriginal State being sovereign and autonomous in our community, government, development, culture and law, and[35]
- agree that all Aboriginal hunting, fishing, camping and usufructuary rights continue without constraint.[36]

To Indigenous people, land remains:

---

34   P Behrendt, 1995, p 399.
35   Attwood and Markus, 1999, p 311.
36   Attwood and Markus, 1999, p 311.

- a way of protecting culture;
- a means of economic independence; and
- a vehicle for political autonomy.

The economic basis for this land is also intricately wound up in the central place that land plays in the Indigenous rights debate. Consider the following from Mandawuy Yunupingu, a member of the Yothu Yindi Foundation:

> In terms of land management, I see a lot more interaction between Aboriginal and non-Aboriginal people, both on a federal and state level. Aboriginal people are again starting to get themselves involved in various aspects of land management, such as conservation. I see Aboriginal and non-Aboriginal people working towards that ... We would include mining companies and all the people who have a vested interest in the resources of this country, and work with them to manage land. If mining is to be allowed by Aboriginal people on their land, they are obviously going to have to be involved with the management so that precautions can be taken to ensure that conservation is part of the whole process. Through this involvement, Aboriginal people are going to participate more in today's commercial world.[37]

Included in rights to land are hunting rights, fishing rights, water rights and sea rights. Where land has been lost, there is a demand for restitution or compensation.

The protection of cultural practices and customary laws

Recurring themes through claims for sovereignty and self-determination are the protection of cultural practices and heritage and, as a corollary, the protection of customary law. Charles Perkins explains the important role cultural practice and cultural heritage:

> To survive as a nation within Australia we must re-establish our Aboriginal cultural base throughout Australia. Aboriginal culture is the *raison d'être* for our existence. It was our anchor in the past. It should be our anchor in the future. It provides the purpose and the passion. It should be our uniting force. We need our culture, to bring us together once again as a people. Today we are divided and disorganised. There has never been so much bitterness between

---

37 M Yunupingu, 1994, 'Give Back Our Laws', *Herald Sun*, 25 January, p 4.

Aboriginal people as there is today. We fight like hungry black dogs over a diminishing budgetary bone thrown to us by our white and black manipulators![38]

Indigenous people express the need to live their lives the way that they want to. This is an assertion of the distinctiveness of Indigenous culture, of the authentic self, even where it has been metamorphosed by the urban environment. The ultimate goal is the creation of a space that allows the enjoyment of a cultural lifestyle, an environment that allows individuals to enjoy their religious and cultural customs and activities, another way of asserting control and participating and taking control of decision-making processes.

Related to this and a recurrent theme of cultural protection through the articulation of the recognition of sovereignty and the exercise of self-determination is the need for the recognition of customary law. To quote again from the draft treaty written by Kevin Gilbert in consultation with Aboriginal Members of the Sovereign Aboriginal Coalition:

> Let it be clearly understood that the Aboriginal position on Land Rights is a Sovereign Aboriginal Position. From the Beginning of Time, time immemorial, our people, our culture, our land areas were clearly defined in the law and have so remained. The Aboriginal Law was not available to vagaries of change and 'amendment'. The Law was, and remains, a constant and unchanging law of rights, duties and responsibilities. [39]

Equal protection of rights

Claims to sovereignty also include claims to protection of rights as they have been identified as universal human rights under international law. These claims highlight the fact that Indigenous people are aware that their rights are less protected than other people in Australia – they demand equality, understanding that all are entitled to the human rights articulated under the international human rights instruments. This was made very clear in the Barunga statement where reference is made to certain universal human rights as entrenched in human rights instruments:

---

38 Perkins, 1994, p 37.
39 Attwood and Markus, 1999, p 310.

(in accordance with the Universal Declaration on Human Rights, the International Covenant on Economic, Social, and Cultural Rights, the International Covenant on Civil and Political Rights, and the Convention for the Elimination of all forms of Racial Discrimination) rights to life, liberty, security of person, food, clothing, housing, medical care, education and employment opportunities, necessary social services and other basic rights.[40]

The parameters of Indigenous claims: Some conclusions

The debate over Indigenous empowerment through sovereignty and self-determination has become stymied, even amongst sympathetic parties, through the semantic confusion over the use of the term sovereignty and what expressions of self-determination might mean. Non-Indigenous Australians have not understood the substance of what it is that Indigenous people are asking for in their political agenda and have reacted defensively to words like sovereignty. Faced with defensive responses to the term sovereignty, Indigenous people have been confined by their inability to communicate their political agenda to the rest of Australia.

Indigenous people need to be given the space to allow the expression and articulation of their needs and political aspirations. There is a need for self-reflection on both sides and the need for improved dialogue between Indigenous and non-Indigenous people.

Recognition of sovereignty and the exercise of self-determination: A listing

What emerges is the idea of the recognition of sovereignty as an expression of distinct identity and a starting point for the exercise of self-determination as a way of achieving empowerment, autonomy and equality. By pinpointing some of the recurrent themes in the recognition of sovereignty and the exercise of self-determination, it is possible to see where these aspirations have found form in current debates.

- *Recognition of Past Injustices*
  - Changing national identity
  - Reconciliation

---

40   The Barunga statement, reproduced in I Moores (ed), 1995, p 332.

- Preamble to the Constitution
- Treaty
- *Autonomy and Decision-Making*
  - Decentralised government
  - Economic base
  - Recognition of customary laws
  - Regional framework agreement
- *Property Rights and Compensation*
  - Recognition of land rights
  - Recognition of other property rights
  - Compensation
  - Non-discrimination in dealings with land
  - Allow development of culture and more modern uses
  - Hunting and fishing
  - Sea and river rights
  - Right to negotiate
  - Oral evidence
- *Protection of Cultural Practices and Customary Laws*
  - Customary laws
  - Institutional experimentation
  - Heritage protection
- *Equal Protection of Rights*
  - Constitutional protection
  - Bill of Rights

What becomes clear is that there is a spectrum of rights that are included in the recognition of sovereignty and the exercise of self-determination. The above categorisation is deceptive in that the rights identified are more complexly interrelated than a checklist makes them appear. The recognition of property rights is necessary for the protection of cultural heritage; autonomy and self-government are related to economic self-sufficiency which is again linked to the recognition of property rights but also an essential prerequisite to the recognition of customary law. Among those rights, some require fundamental changes to the structure of Australian society, some could be achieved with legislation and others should already be recognised.

This agenda aims at increased decision-making processes, an aspiration 'to live my life my way'. Although there may be some confusion among non-Indigenous Australians about what the terms sovereignty and self-determination actually mean, they are clearly identifiable aspirations on the Indigenous political agenda, even if the details of how they might apply to differing circumstances are not yet fleshed out. In fact, recognition of Indigenous sovereignty and the exercise of self-determination offer a remedy to continuing tension between Indigenous and non-Indigenous people. They offer an agenda for inclusion, participation and equality and an agenda for deconstruction, redistribution, reconstruction and institutional change.

These agendas, this recognition and these tools for self-determination need to lead to structural change to destabilise the psychological *terra nullius* that infects Australia's institutions. A program that does not have a goal of institutional change at its heart will not alter the entrenched bias and ideologies entrenched in institutional structures. Such a program of institutional change will be the subject of the next chapter.

Chapter 5
New strategies, improved rights protection

On 12 August, 2000, Noel Pearson, former Chairperson of the Cape York Land Council, delivered the Ben Chifley Memorial Lecture. In it, he criticised the way in which welfare dependency had kept Indigenous people in a subordinate position. Three days later, Geoff Clark, as Chair of ATSIC, announced that he would seek an extra $245 million a year to be allocated to Indigenous health from the then Health Minister, Dr Michael Wooldridge, over the next four years. Mr Clark added that he would alert Dr Wooldridge to a $4 billion shortfall in infrastructure, such as housing.[1] These two seemingly contradictory strategies caused one reader of the *Sydney Morning Herald* to write a letter to the editor.

> Could Noel Pearson, and Geoff Clark, as portrayed in today's *Herald* be representatives of the same people? Pearson's so poignant and positive — as aligned to Clark's bellicosity. A mere $245 million extra per year, plus an additional $4 billion for housing. I think John Winston will be moved to say, sorry.[2]

However, if one looks past the media sound bites, it becomes clear that both Indigenous leaders share a similar vision. They are emphasising different aspects of what should be conceptualised as a complementary agenda rather than, as often portrayed, conflicting and oppositional ones. Noel Pearson was not arguing for the abolition of welfare — as some conservative critics declared — but for the reform of the welfare system to enhance the economic self-sufficiency of Indigenous communities. Elsewhere Pearson has stated:

---

1 D Jopson, 2000, 'Vote of confidence, now Clark battles on', *Sydney Morning Herald,* 16 August, p 4.
2 Letter to the Editor, *Sydney Morning Herald.* 18 August 2000, p 15.

The state is reluctant to transfer responsibility to people on the ground. Because the state holds all the resources, it is the powerful party, and whilst the state desires to solve social problems, its inherent methods are frequently the source of the problem ... We must ensure that government does not continue to deliver negative welfare and operate in the modes and mentalities of negative welfare, and we must ensure that government programs on the ground become holistic.[3]

One of Pearson's main aims is to ensure decision-making power is returned to a regional community level. It is through this arrangement that the specific and pressing needs of the Indigenous community can be more adequately met. He has also expressed frustration at the focus on broader rights issues at the expense of the very real and urgent life-and-death issues that face Indigenous communities in his area of Cape York.

This economic and political self-sufficiency has been the political aim of Geoff Clark, very vocally so in his advocacy work with the Aboriginal Provisional Government (APG). Both men are community-based leaders — Pearson in Cape York and Clark in Framlingham (Victoria) — who understand the need for economic self-sufficiency in the long-term but the short-term need for funds and welfare. Both have strong grass-roots affiliations and are known for their visionary forward-looking contributions while understanding the immediate needs of Indigenous people in their day-to-day lives.

What seems to have become confused is the fact that outside observers think that the options are either getting people off welfare or increasing welfare. With over 200 years of colonisation and with entrenched racism and colonial ideologies in Australia's institutions, it is surprising that anyone considering a solution to Indigenous socio-economic disadvantage would think that there is one simple cure-all to the myriad of problems, issues and aspirations faced and held by Indigenous communities. Indigenous leaders understand that there are no simple, one-step solutions and that is why suggested mechanisms for improving rights include the multifaceted approach of immediate relief matched with long-term economic goals.

However, what is often not clear — or made clear — is how these different approaches work together. In this chapter, I want to outline a program for institutional change that seeks to achieve the aspirations identified in the previous chapter. This approach is designed to give a

---

3   N Pearson, 2000, 'Aboriginal Disadvantage', in M Grattan (ed), *Reconciliation*, Black Ink, p 170.

structured sense of how rights protection can be achieved. It concentrates on the need for thoughtful, strategic approaches to rights protection that adopt both the short-term and long-term approaches advocated by community leaders such as Noel Pearson and Geoff Clark, and seeks to ensure that such changes are structural *and* institutional.

Pearson emphasised the structural element in his Ben Chifley Memorial Lecture. 'There are *structural* reasons why we occupy the lowest most dismal place in the underclass of Australian society. There are structural reasons why all our efforts to rise up and to improve our situation are constantly impeded.'

Structural change is important because it attacks the ideologies, the psychological *terra nullius*, which make institutions seem neutral. In addition, Indigenous Australians are seeking a transformation of the state and their autonomy, place and role within it. Since formal equality as a model for the recognition of rights has failed to bring Indigenous Australians the same enjoyment of rights as other Australians and has not created the space that members of this cultural group need to express their cultural distinctiveness, the challenge becomes finding ways to improve democratic institutions and explore alternative institutional frameworks.

A program for institutional change

Society treats existing institutions and principles as conclusions, not as one of many possible alternatives. This limitation in understanding the possibilities for alternative institutional arrangements 'blocks personal curiosity, organises public memory, and heroically imposes certainty on uncertainty.'[4] This conception of structural change seeks imaginative institutional alternatives.

In developing the following framework, I make two assumptions.

- Individuals have the power to transform and transcend institutions.
- Tinkering with institutions can lead to radical changes in institutional forms.

---

4   M Douglas, 1986, *How Institutions Think*, Syracuse University Press, p 102. Douglas observes that institutions 'control the memory of its members; it causes them to forget experiences incompatible with its righteous image, and it brings to their minds events which sustain the view of nature that is complementary to itself. It provides the categories of their thought, sets the terms for self-knowledge and fixes categories': p 112.

This means that I assume that we are bigger than the institutions that shape our lives and that we have the ability to change the institutions in the society in which we live. Social theorist Mary Douglas notes that individuals are greater than institutions since '[a]n institution cannot have purposes. Only individuals can intend, plan consciously, and contrive oblique strategies.'[5] She adds: 'For us, the hope of intellectual independence is to resist, and the necessary first step in resistance is to discover how the institutional grip is laid upon our mind.'[6]

This picks up on Roberta Sykes' notion of personal sovereignty and that of Michael Mansell,[7] that Indigenous people can, need to and should 'act' in a sovereign manner.

> On what basis today are we Aboriginal people prepared to give up our right to control ourselves and our lands? In my view, we consent to it! We give our consent to people outside of our communities to control us, our lands, and our communities. We do so by the way we conduct ourselves, our behaviour, all of which amounts to allowing white people to make all the important decisions. We respond to the consequences of those important decisions. Someone said to me yesterday: 'Why doesn't the Australian government give us self-determination?' The easy answer is that we have never asked for it; we have never demanded it. What we have said to the Australian government is: 'You have a right to make all the important decisions — we will talk about the little nitty-gritty decisions that flow from it.' We need to challenge our own views; we need to question the way in which we have looked at these issues in the past.[8]

I also assume that small changes — tinkering — with institutions can lead to broader, more profound and fundamental changes in the long term if those small changes are strategic.

By assuming this, Indigenous people can strategically move towards long-term goals, working on what is achievable in the more immediate future and seeing each point as a step in a trajectory towards a certain long-term aspiration. This matching needs to be with an understanding of what is achievable in the short term, what is

---

5   Douglas, 1986, p 92.
6   Douglas, 1986, p 92.
7   Legal Manager, Tasmanian Aboriginal Legal Centre.
8   M Mansell, 1994, 'Taking Control of Resources', in C Fletcher (ed), *Aboriginal Self-Determination in Australia*, Australian Institute of Aboriginal and Torres Strait Islander Studies, p 162.

achievable in the long term and mapping how to get from one point to the next. This is not a new concept but one that Michael Mansell identified several years ago:

> We need to be conscious of the future, but we also need to secure the present. I have consistently argued that, whatever it is that is offered to you by governments, grab hold of it; if it is a welfare package — grab it; if it is a piece of legislation and you think it might be of benefit to your community — grab it; if you believe that entrenching your rights in the constitution will bring about benefit and change — grab it. But, we must be sure that we do not put governments in a position where they can use our desire for short-term benefits against our long-term development.[9]

The move towards structural change will lead to a transcendence of the current institutional framework and will produce a deeper change to the fabric of Australian society and will facilitate changes to the socio-economic position of Indigenous Australians as institutions become more democratic and inclusive, not just for Indigenous people but for all Australians.

Agency

If we assume that people are greater than institutions, institutional change needs to have an agent. Members of excluded and disadvantaged minorities can be effective in this role, as they feel alienated by the institutions of their society — the legal system, the Constitution, government structures — and do not have the loyalty to them that the better-off in society do. As people who are part of the state but treated as 'other', Indigenous people have less vested in current institutional arrangements. For historical and cultural reasons, Indigenous people are uniquely positioned to make effective agents for change. Indigenous people express a cynicism towards existing institutional arrangements and do not have as much invested in idealised institutions as other sectors of the community. There is an understanding that bias occurs in the criminal justice systems and that there is racism in policy-making. Ideologies and bias entrenched in the state apparatus work against Indigenous people so they have the least to lose from a restructuring or an alternative institutional regime. Further, Australian institutions do not always reflect Indigenous cultural values. Indigenous people are therefore exposed to different

---

9   Mansell, 1994, p 164.

canons and live between two different cultures — the dominant and the Indigenous — and so have more contexts in which to explore options and ways of understanding. By walking between two cultural lines, Indigenous people are already familiar with the idea that there are different ways of approaching institutions.

There is clear evidence of this agency through the involvement of Indigenous people at a grass-roots level when policies fail. It can be seen in the work of Indigenous women who set up drying out areas, medical services and Indigenous women's legal services. It can be seen in members of the community who set up legal services, housing cooperatives and who work together to buy the community hall or the community bus. In addition, the presence of more Indigenous people in the 'mainstream' has meant the gradual change of perspectives and alteration of institutional culture in some areas, particularly in relation to policy development in the National Parks and Wildlife Services. It can also be seen in curriculum changes in schools and tertiary institutions.

Indigenous rights and aspirations

In the previous chapter, I attempted to identify a spectrum of rights recurrent in claims to sovereignty and self-determination under the following headings.

- Recognition of past injustices
- Autonomy and decision-making
- Property rights and compensation
- Protection of cultural practices and customary laws
- Equal protection of rights

I want to explore how aspirations may be strategically placed in a project of institutional change to achieve greater protection of Indigenous rights. This is aided by looking at the spectrum of rights and noting that some should already be protected (non-discrimination) and others would require structural change (alternative institutional arrangements). Some could occur quite quickly (changes to native title legislation) while others would require a detailed process of consultation and formal processes (a treaty, constitutional change). Below I have attempted to identify how these goals could be mapped on trajectories in an attempt to make some links between these issues.

ACHIEVING SOCIAL JUSTICE

Urgent issues	Rights framework	
	Short term	**Long term**
	Symbolic recognition →	Preamble to the Constitution
Welfare reform	Treaty making process →	Treaty
	Education	The national self-image
Family violence		
	Affirmative action programs	Economic redistribution
Health	Protection of property rights	
Education		
Housing	Cultural practice	Alternative institutional forms
	Customary law	
Employment	Delegation of power →	Regional framework agreements
	Alliance building →	A more energised politics
	Legislative bill of rights	Constitutional protection
	International rights protection	

Urgent issues column annotations:
- Ongoing commitment to targeted and identified policy making
- Directed at the urgent day-to-day needs of Indigenous people and communities

It is important to note that these various options for long-term structural change work side-by-side with the continuing targeting of policy areas of urgent and pressing need for Indigenous communities — health, education, employment, reduction of violence levels. The pursuit of a rights agenda should be seen as a co-existing and complementary strategy to those targeted policy areas. An improved rights framework with strengthen the effectiveness of policy development and implementation because it will assist in establishing mechanisms for greater Indigenous input and control over policy-making. It will also ensure mechanisms for improved rights protection that result from better targeted and more strategic policy. It will guide policy-making to consider not just short-term solutions but strategic long-term goals. This will allow policies to deliver longer term, rather than merely reactive, solutions.

In the next chapter, I want to draw out three examples of these short-term and long-term steps but first I want to note three underlying principles that should direct the pursuit, development and implementation of the institutional and structural reforms. They are not an exhaustive list of such principles but they are essential to guide a strategic process of institutional change.

Some underlying principles

There are three thematic principles important to the institutional change that I want to identify:

- *Substantive equality*: measuring outcomes rather than accepting the notion of formal equality
- *Effective participation*: broad and influential inclusion in decision-making processes
- *Legal pluralism*: the acceptance of the co-existence of institutional forms

Substantive equality

Principles of justice, fairness and equity run through the ideological foundations of almost every society. These principles are the catch-cries of freedom, written into constitutions and the centrepiece of any modern legal system. It is not the *desire* of these principles which causes tension — most Australians would say that they agree with the idea of equality and non-discrimination — but it is *how* those principles can be achieved and their success measured that is controversial.

Rights conferred on members of a community should be applied to all segments of society equally. However, equality needs to be measured not by the existence of a rights framework but by assessing the end result of the framework. The focus needs to be on what happens *after* the institutions and ideals are placed on society, not on how it looks in the abstract.

It is perhaps the biggest indictment on Australia's institutions that many of the rights that Indigenous people are seeking are ones that other Australians unquestioningly enjoy. Rights to medical treatment, education and food feature prominently in the claims of Indigenous rights. Australia has signed and ratified all major international human rights documents that promote the protection of equal rights for all and list a universal understanding of what those basic human rights are.

Many of the injustices suffered by Indigenous people today flow from a model of formal equality, the application of 'same laws', but leading to disparate impacts and disparate outcomes.

Patrick Dodson made the following observation.

> Aborigines have never wanted to be the same as the white man. What we have sought is to have substantial equality so that as human beings there might be a quality of life that we can enjoy in keeping with our own values and societal ways. Lives for our peoples, similar to that of the majority in Australia but lives uniquely ours, not ones that governments wished to impose upon us. Lives where we meet out obligations as citizens but where we are accommodated also as Aborigines. Lives where our human and cultural rights are respected by the governments that have told the world they would respect them.[10]

A model of substantive equality recognises there is no even playing field and no institutional neutrality and encourages critical assessment of institutions while encouraging exploration of alternative institutional arrangements. Because substantive equality is concerned with the equality of outcomes, it allows for a balancing of equal measures with special measures, a balance that allows difference and equality to co-exist. It means measuring the success of legal reforms, legislation

---

10 P Dodson, 2000, 'Beyond the Mourning Gate — Dealing with Unfinished Business', 12th Wentworth Lecture, Australian Institute of Aboriginal and Torres Strait Islander Studies, p 14.

and policies by their ability to create equality. This results-oriented approach rejects formal equality unless it can produce equality in its outcomes.

Effective participation

Indigenous people may have been granted symbolic inclusion into Australian society with the 1967 Referendum but representing just over 2 per cent of the population, it has been difficult for Aboriginal and Torres Strait Islander people to create the political pressure necessary to initiate changes that might lead to an improvement in socio-economic positions, greater autonomy and structural change.

There are two problems with creating representative government for Indigenous people aside from low numbers in the overall population. Any political action is dependant upon these two factors.

- The gaining of popular support from the rest of the community to allow enough pressure to be brought to bear on political representatives
- The gaining of consensus within the community on what strategy to take. Communities are diverse and have very different, often conflicting needs so a united front is not always easy to achieve.

Effective participation has the dual goals of promoting group association and addressing underlying social disadvantage through involvement in decision-making processes. These twin goals seek to facilitate representative decision-making in decentralised political units in order to develop models of political participation that allow for more effective representation at the local level as well as to promote arrangements that allow individuals who are members of minority groups to have real influence in the public arena. Effective participation seeks to increase decision-making power by including members of minority groups in the mechanisms of the dominant culture as well as ensuring increased decision-making ability at a local level by increased self-government mechanisms.

This participation goes to the heart of the universal right of self-determination as defined by international law. Under international law, the principle of self-determination has been interpreted as promoting a standard of legitimacy against which institutions of government are to be measured. S James Anaya has deconstructed the concept of internal self-determination, identifying the substantive aspects of legitimate government that it seeks to promote and protect.[11] Anaya identifies two main features within these substantive aspects.

- A *constitutive* aspect: that self-determination requires any governing institutional order to be substantially the creation of processes guided by the will of the people(s) governed.
- An *ongoing* aspect: that self-determination requires that a governing institutional order, independent of the processes leading to its creation or alteration, be one under which people may live and develop freely on a continuous basis.[12]

The *constitutive* aspect of self-determination creates a standard that requires that any creation of or change in institutions of governance within any given sphere of the community must be done with the participation and consent of *all* members of the public. This creates a standard of legitimacy against which original social contracts and subsequent nation-building practices can be measured. The *ongoing* aspect imposes a standard under which individuals and groups are able to make meaningful choices within governance structures under which they live in matters touching upon all spheres of life on a continuous basis. This understands that self-determination is an ongoing process, requiring constant monitoring and reassessment of its effectiveness.

Participation in politics is a central pillar in notions of democracy and an important aspect in the right to self-determination. Where there has been exclusion from society by one sector of the community, there is not just a violation of the right to self-determination but a questioning of the legitimacy of the state both in its creation and its ongoing operation.

This goal to increase participation needs to be pursued through projects which emphasise participation through alliance building and political mobilisation. This participation can be facilitated by:

- alliance-building with other minority and excluded groups;
- developing a strong political front and a well-defined agenda; and
- inclusion, through affirmative action programs of members of minority groups in all aspects of the decision-making process.

This notion of nation-building finds fault with the current Australian state because of its inability from its inception to have included the

---

11 S James Anaya, 1996, *Indigenous Peoples in International Law*, Oxford University Press.
12 Anaya, 1996, p 81.

perspective and obtained the consent of Indigenous people. It didn't occur at the time of invasion. It didn't occur at Federation. As the *Mabo* case illustrates, the question of the validity of British acquisition of Australia is still one that has not been adequately answered and it also leaves a question mark over the legal legitimacy of the modern Australian state. A belated nation-building process, one that ensured the greater inclusion of Indigenous people in the decision-making processes that affects the lives of all Australians, would see a new relationship develop that would bring Indigenous peoples into the state on new terms.

Legal pluralism

Legal pluralism is the existence of different legal orders within the same jurisdiction. There is a spectrum of ways in which the law can seek to accommodate difference and otherness.

- *One set of laws which takes into account cultural differences*: Some attempt has been made to include cultural differences and practices within the existing legal system to ameliorate individual instances of inequality. These remedial measures take several different forms:
- cross-cultural training programs aimed to educate professionals such as the judiciary;
- training of Indigenous people as lawyers, police and other professional positions;
- taking into account the Indigenous perspective when interacting with an Indigenous person, such as in sentencing;
- remedial legislation that prohibits and provides remedies for specific cases of discrimination in the public sphere such as the *Racial Discrimination Act* 1975 (Cth).

These methods may alleviate cultural conflict or bias but they do nothing to stop the source of those cultural conflicts. For example, there are cross-cultural training programs designed to make court officers, officials, judges and mediators more sympathetic towards Indigenous defendants who are brought before their jurisdiction. This is done on the principle that some education in Indigenous culture and experience will alleviate cultural conflict. Cultural sensitivity training seeks to cushion the institutional/cultural clash, leaving in place institutional structures that are prejudicial to Indigenous peoples rather than remedying the conflict by providing alternative institutional arrangements.

Similarly, the inclusion of Indigenous people within the legal system in roles as Justices of the Peace, lawyers and judges works on the premise that the sight of Indigenous faces on the bench and in the courtroom might make the Indigenous defendant feel more at ease, that it will lessen cultural conflict and bias.[13] However, this approach does nothing to alleviate the socio-economic problems that cause Indigenous people to be over-represented in the court system in the first place and, while it may provide for a more understanding hearing, it does little to change institutional structures and their entrenched, neo-colonial ideologies.[14] Something more substantive than tinkering within legal and political institutions is required in order to remove the power imbalance within the legal structure.

- *Two Systems of Laws and Institutional Experimentalism*

    The concepts of substantive equality and effective participation recognise that institutional arrangements are loaded with bias and ideology. To counter those entrenched ideologies and biases, institutions need to be subverted and transformed. There are two ways to approach this institutional change.

- *The recognition of customary law*

    The recognition of customary law is designed to take into account distinct cultural values and perspectives; a more equal playing field can be established by the recognition within existing institutions of existing cultural practices. It is usually in pockets of the existing legal system that allowances will be made to accommodate customary practices in places where recognition of a cultural practice will not affect institutional structures such as the recognition of traditional marriages.

---

13 See generally, L Behrendt, 1995, *Aboriginal Dispute Resolution*, Federation Press, especially Chapters 4 and 5.

14 See J Behrendt and L Behrendt, 1992b, 'Aborigines and the Police: Bad Apples or Rotten Fruit?', *Tharunka* vol 38, issue 4, 14 April, pp 14-15. The RCIADIC noted that there was an over-representation in the number of Indigenous people who were brought into the local courts on charges under the NSW *Crimes Act* 1900 because they had used offensive language to police officers. Pat O'Shane, an Indigenous magistrate, was dismissive of such cases brought before her, understanding that it was a manifestation of the police disdain for Indigenous people in the Redfern area. An ABC report managed to document those abuses on videotape taken from within police cars. It showed police officers using overtly racist names to describe Indigenous people they saw on the streets then jump out of the police cars and arrest them for offensive language.

NEW STRATEGIES, IMPROVED RIGHTS PROTECTION

- *The institutional embodiment of differences in institutional forms*
  Indigenous practice, customs and values could be a starting point for new institutional arrangements. Real cultural difference can be the seeds to the creation of new institutions and the facilitation of the real innovation that needs to take place within Australia's legal and social institutions. These new institutions would not just be aimed at distinct cultural groups but used in the wider communities. By developing institutions based on alternative values and procedures, designed to include Indigenous people, those structures will also include other alienated sectors of the community whose cultural values might more closely align with those of the Indigenous culture. It is in this sphere that the greatest hope for innovative institutional experimentation takes place.

It is within this last option that seeks the creation of legal pluralism and institutional experimentation that entrenched institutional ideologies and biases can be countered. It is this promise of institutional experimentation that provides the greatest hope for a more inclusive society.

◆ ◆ ◆

The failure of institutions to provide for the effective recognition of rights for Indigenous people — rights that all Australians are entitled to — highlights a fundamental weakness in Australia's democratic structure. Improving society means reforming it — and acknowledging that any program for improvement *must* be concerned with institutional arrangements. The Indigenous experience has shown that working *within* existing institutional forms leaves the ideologies and biases which infest those institutional structures unchanged. Restructuring a society to create substantive equality and effective political participation requires a program of institutional change that will alter and transform existing institutional arrangements, and attack the causes of bias and cultural conflict. The principles of *substantive equality* and *effective participation* work towards a society that recognises the importance of individual choices and the importance of the communal context. Both principles require a questioning of institutional arrangements and an opportunity to explore institutional pluralism in order to counter the entrenched bias and ideologies in canonical institutions.

Chapter 6

Towards improved rights protection: Some first steps and some alternative futures

Initial steps towards improved rights protection and self determination requiring only policy or legislative changes to implement were identified in the previous chapter:
- symbolic recognition
- a treaty-making process
- improving education
- improving affirmative action programs
- strengthening Indigenous property rights
- the protection of cultural practice and the recognition of customary law
- delegation of power
- alliance building
- a bill of rights
- increased rights protection under international law

This is by no means an exhaustive list. While these first steps require little or no alteration to existing laws, each works towards visionary aims that require structural or constitutional change. These longer-term aspirational initiatives that lead to institutional change which will facilitate greater rights protection and the exercise of self-determination and include:
- a preamble to the Constitution
- a treaty
- the national self-image
- economic redistribution

- alternative institutional forms
- regional framework agreements
- a more energised politics
- Constitutional protection

Far from being simply the agenda for a special interest group, this project of improved rights protection is based on transforming Australian society in a manner that produces widespread reform and redistribution, creating benefits for other marginalised and socio-economically disadvantaged groups.

I do not propose to deal with each of the possible trajectories identified above. Instead, I will canvas three of these issues in order to give a sense of the possible pathways forward and to suggest appropriate aspirational goals with the hope that it might spark further debate, investigation and research. These are trajectories towards:

- a *new national self-image*: because of the importance of overturning Australia's psychological *terra nullius*;
- *constitutional change*: because proposals for altering the Constitution play such a prominent role in suggestions for improving Indigenous rights protections;
- *regional autonomy*: because the decentralisation of power to Indigenous communities embraces the concept of self-determination.

Towards a new national self-Image

Symbolic recognition

Symbolic recognition goes to the heart of the recognition of past injustices such as denial of sovereignty, dispossession and the child removal policy. It may take many forms:

- a national apology by the Prime Minister recognising past injustices and the effect that they continue to have on Indigenous people;
- memorials marking places of past injustices such as massacre sites and acknowledging traditional owners;
- observance of protocols such as acknowledgment of traditional owners and 'welcome to country';
- references in the preambles of legislative acts concerning Aboriginal and Torres Strait Islander people;
- the flying of the Aboriginal and Torres Strait Islander flags.

These small reminders, acknowledgments and displays of respect seek to incorporate Indigenous experience, history and presence into the Australian psyche. It is a symbolic recognition readily acknowledged in other sectors. Historian Henry Reynolds makes this point.

> White Australians frequently say 'all that' should be forgotten. But it will not be. It cannot be. Black memories are too deeply, too recently scarred. And forgetfulness is a strange prescription coming from a community that has revered the fallen warrior and emblazoned the phrase 'Lest We Forget' on monuments throughout the land.[1]

Reynolds also warns of the continued alienation of Indigenous people from Australian society and its institutions if such acknowledgment is not made.

> In the long run black Australians will be our equals or our enemies. Unless they can identify with new and radical interpretations of our history they will seek sustenance in the anti-colonial traditions of the third world. If they are unable to find a place of honour in the white man's story of the past their loyalties will increasingly dwell with the 'wretched of the earth'.[2]

The recognition of past injustices may seem tokenistic and not very useful if a symbolic recognition is not accompanied by substantive rights. However, even symbolic gestures have consequences that could have profound effects on the relationship that Indigenous people have with the rest of Australia.

- They restore dignity to Indigenous people that is fundamental to self-respect and a feeling of acceptance.
- Recognition of the treatment of Indigenous people and the true story of how Australia was invaded will have a profound effect on Australia's national identity.
- Recognition of sovereignty and prior ownership by Indigenous people may eventually lead to more substantive changes, including legal reforms, as the assumptions and mindsets of decision-makers, law-makers and policy-makers shift.

These effects also assist in reshaping notions of Australian nationalism, redefining the power relation within Australia and assisting the erosion of the intolerance, ignorance, negative stereotypes and

---

1 H Reynolds, 1982, *The Other Side of the Frontier: Aboriginal Resistance to the European Invasion of Australia*, Penguin, p 201.
2 Reynolds, 1982, p 199.

overt racism prevalent in Australian society that work to alienate members of the Indigenous community. This will provide an environment more conducive to substantial protection of rights.

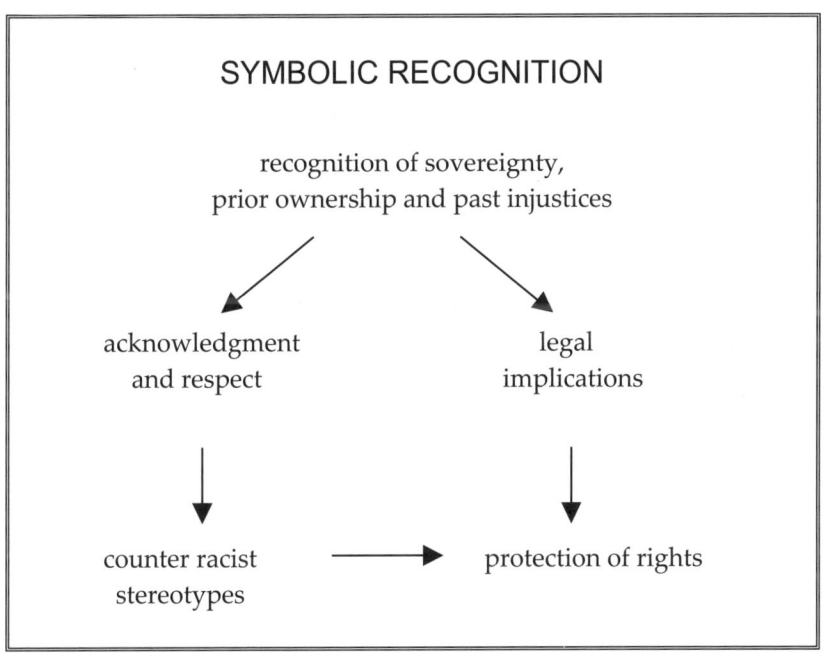

This symbolic recognition provides a basis for nation-building that will 'tear at the legacies of empire, discrimination, suppression of democratic participation, and cultural suffocation.'[3] By overturning Australia's psychological *terra nullius* through the recognition of Indigenous presence, it will thus works towards a new, more inclusive sense of being Australian. Symbolic gestures will provide an environment in which there is an understanding of historical legacies and a willingness to alleviate the effects of past injustices. This atmosphere will create a societal climate conducive to the acceptance and protection of Indigenous rights.

---

3   Anaya, 1996, p 75.

Improving education

Wadjularbinna Nulyarimma, a Ganggalida spokesperson from Doomadgee, has said:

> First of all you have to learn about us. Education has been a one-way street for 205 years. Learn about us and what makes us tick. Accept that we *are* different. Don't try to make us into white people. Accept us and respect us as you are expecting us to respect you. *You* respect us with our differences and we'll respect *you*. We can live in harmony in this country despite all the things you have been doing to make people go into the mainstream — once people are recognised as the people we *are* then reconciliation will follow automatically and all these colleges and universities, all the doors won't be able to hold my people. They'll go through them because they'll feel good about themselves. They'll identify as the people who have lived here for thousands of years. They'll have so much to contribute they'll walk through those doors in pride. That is the secret of the change that must take place in this country.[4]

Wadjularbinna Nulyarimma identifies two aspects about education.

- non-Indigenous Australians need to learn about Indigenous Australians;
- as Indigenous people come to feel more included in the education system, they will perform better.

The reform of educational institutions is the first step in a long-term project for countering inequality and exclusion of minority and disadvantaged groups. It provides a way to confront the agents of racism that are outside the reach of affirmative action projects. This reform of education becomes a two-pronged attack based on Wadjularbinna Nulyarimma's observation. Its aims are:

- the development of an environment conducive to changing perceptions and facilitating tolerance for difference (*content*); and
- the opportunity to provide better education to excluded minorities, such as Indigenous people, so that they do not need to rely on affirmative action programs but can enter institutions on their own terms avoiding tokenism (*access*).

The experience of Indigenous families with the practices of the Aborigines Protection Board (APB) makes the prospect of more state

---

4 W Nulyarimma, interview with Caroline Jones, reproduced in I Moores (ed), *Voices of Aboriginal Australia: Past, Present, Future*, (Butterfly Books, 1995), p 421.

control over a child a frightening one. The fear is that the child will become instilled with European values, be belittled for following Aboriginal and Torres Strait Islander cultural practices and become assimilated into the dominant culture. This is a danger within the education system that exists in Australia presently, one which embodies a history and tradition of white supremacy. This would not be the case if the values of the education system were changed to be more inclusive and the role of the education system was one that develops the potential of all children given to its care by offering a broad range of canons, opportunities and perspectives.

This can only be achieved through an uncoupling of a national identity from the institutions of the state. The school should not be a sphere of indoctrination but a realm of exploration of capabilities and alternatives. The education of a child should emphasise the development of his or her abilities, not the ideologies of the dominant culture. This allows a child to develop in an environment where imagination is fostered and individuality is valued.

As part of achieving this change in educational institutions, there needs to be a reconceptualisation of what has traditionally been thought of as the canons of education systems — canons that usually reflect the values of the dominant culture. The recognition of a multiplicity of canons will allow for the acknowledgment of racial experiences, teach the value of difference and allow children from previously excluded groups to feel that their difference is appreciated and important. For example, there is a tradition of telling history only from 1788 when the first Europeans settled in Australia and omitting the experiences of Indigenous Australia resulting from invasion and colonisation. Indigenous children have felt excluded from the education system because of this failure to recognise their history and experience. In turn, non-Indigenous children are left ignorant of their own history and consequently may be prejudiced towards 'others' due to their lack of understanding. Educational reform that allows for the teaching of other perspectives is one way that an atmosphere of fostering difference and tolerance could be achieved.

Such reform needs to be coupled with the reform of the methodological canons that are used in schools. Allowing children to become more active in the way that they learn will spark their imaginations. It will allow children who do not respond well to the current academic teaching practices to excel under alternative teaching methods. This can give them a better chance of unlocking their talents and a greater sense of confidence, both of which will make them more useful members of society. More specifically, these changes could include the implementation of the following ways to present experiences and perspectives that differ from those of the dominant culture:

- the writings and other works of Indigenous people that describe Indigenous experience, perspectives and world views;
- lessons in ecology that describe Indigenous methods of land care and create a better understanding of the delicate issues that surround the environment;
- learning history from the perspective of Indigenous people;
- using teaching methods that are creative and flexible, such as story telling as a way of teaching morals, learning from the experiences of Elders, a stronger mentoring system for young people and creating opportunities to learn from experience through field trips, exchange programs and vocational training;
- the establishment of schools that concentrate particularly on Indigenous perspectives and world views.

This kind of transformation of the education system, one that would promote the incorporation of Indigenous people and their history and culture into the school system, could be also utilised by other cultural groups. The same mechanisms for recognition could be afforded to the history of Chinese immigrants in Australia and the values that they have brought to Australia and integrated into their new communities. Reforms based on the greater inclusion of Indigenous perspective and methodology into the education system through the changing of the canon will work towards the changing of the dominant nationalism as children are exposed to balanced versions and perspectives of their history.

Shared histories and a new self-image

Changing society and institutional structures hinges on restructuring what it means to be an Australian and what sort of society Australia should be. It also means coming to terms with the nation's history. This means deconstructing the fictitious (exclusionary) national identity. This reconciliation with the past — a reinterpretation of history — does help to acknowledge past injustices, a recognition that Indigenous Australians are seeking.

History should help Australians understand who they are and how they got to a certain point; history should be a teacher. It should help Australians to assess what they are doing wrong and what they are doing right in a project towards democratic visionary goals.

Australia currently struggles with a notion of national identity. The vision of Australia as a nation of white people is being challenged by a national identity of a multicultural Australia, reflective of its current diversity. This latter interpretation of Australia's nationalism seeks to include previously excluded groups into the Australian psyche.

Clearly this move from a white Australia to multicultural Australia attempts to include all Australians but this interpretation needs to go beyond 'cultural days' where national dress is donned or a new cuisine sampled. Australia must incorporate the experiences and values of other cultures into its society, particularly its institutions. Institutions house certain ideologies. Recognising the ideological content of societal institutions helps to show that a uniform set of institutional arrangements is but *one* possibility in a broad spectrum of institutional possibilities.

Any ideological shift within the Australian community needs to be reflected in its institutions. Institutional reform that embodies *real* differences is critical if it is to incorporate new and inclusive political aspirations and visions, rather than just past ideals.

If Indigenous communities have cultural values that conflict with those of the legal system, those values should be able to form the basis of new value systems embodied in new procedures and new institutions. For example, the communal nature of the Indigenous community is claimed to bring it into conflict with the individual-focused legal system of the current Australian system. Mediation (as an extension of the legal system) reinforces those individual-based values. A more communal approach could be included in the process in a variety of ways:

- allowing family members to address mediators and adjudicators;
- sentencing options that take into account the impact on the family and community;

It is not just the Indigenous communities who feel excluded from the legal process with its focus on the individual. Many cultures have a social weave that is as concentrated on the extended family and community as those of the individual. An institutional model based on Indigenous values of community might be more accommodating to cultural groups who share similar values. This approach allows for the injection of new values into existing institutions and the creation of new institutional forms that reflect the real differences in cultural communities.

Pluralism is more than two laws operating side by side; it recognises that divergence is possible between members of different cultural groups in ways that had not been acknowledged before. It allows one system that is open to everyone, excludes no one, but has different processes and procedures flourishing within it that reflect the diversity of cultural practices within the unit.

Alternatives exist in models that seek to redefine Australia's relationship with its Indigenous people. Although the doctrine of *terra nullius* was overturned in the *Mabo* case, Australia has yet to redress what this new relationship means. By substituting *terra nullius* for the controversial assumption that Australia was 'settled', the High Court did not take the argument about the wrongful acquisition of sovereignty by the British Crown to its logical conclusion. The High Court indicated that the basis for the claim on Australia was erroneous but that the issue was not one that domestic courts could decide. When the High Court did overturn the doctrine of *terra nullius* as an out-of-date legal fiction, it acknowledged that there was a system of law operating at the time of invasion and it acknowledged the continuity of that law when it held that Indigenous customs define native title. Reading between the lines of the court's finding, it can be inferred that there was an acknowledgement that there were Indigenous sovereign nations at the time of the 1788 invasion. The rejection of the myth of *terra nullius* means a rejection of the myth of 'settlement'. It logically follows that if a system of laws and customs existed that recognised native title, that system was a system of governance and sovereignty. The courts have yet to settle this question and their timidity is shared by the reluctance of the broader Australian community to deal with the implications of Indigenous sovereignty.

The British claim to Australia was legally justified through a claim that the land was *terra nullius*.[5] This meant that British imposed

---

5   *Terra nullius* describes a land that is vacant or a land that was without a sovereign. Both premises were incorrect. The Aborigines were certainly there so that negates the first possibility. The issue of there being no sovereign was also one on which the British were (conveniently) misguided. Seeing no chiefs and perceiving a society that was 'inferior' and 'uncivilised', the assumption was made that there was no sovereign. I don't believe that the second reason was really the reason why the land was claimed as *terra nullius*. I think that the British simply wanted the land. They wanted to claim it before the French claimed it and did it in the most convenient way possible. If anything reveals the ludicrous nature of the claim, it is the fact that planting a flag in Botany Bay claimed the whole continent regardless of who or what was on it. The claim of *terra nullius* was deceitful at the time it was made; it was claimed incorrectly under the rules of international law at the time it was made and the British fully understood that.

their legal system on the people of Australia without regard to the law and custom of the Indigenous people. This was erroneous, and the High Court admitted it.[6] The belief that Indigenous people were not Christian and therefore could fall under the sovereignty of the British is reflective of attitudes of the time.

The British claim that they *discovered* Australia has been discredited. International law at the time of colonisation considered that where sovereignty over land was claimed because there was no sovereign, the administration of the territory should be temporary, lasting only such time as the Indigenous people were capable of administering themselves.[7]

An alternative claim of conquest could have been made by the British. Under the rules of international law, they would have had to respect Indigenous laws and Indigenous property rights. Neither happened. A recognition that Australia was a conquered nation could give rise in law to the right of recognition of those customs and property interests, allowing Indigenous people legal leverage in asserting the legitimacy of their property rights and entitling them to the same protection due to all individuals, as well as allowing greater scope for the recognition of customary law.

These unresolved issues of the circumstances of Australia's 'settlement' leave questions about the legitimacy of the Australian state. The resolution of the issues of Indigenous sovereignty and the legal status of British assertions of acquisition of Indigenous land, in the light of the overturning of the doctrine of *terra nullius*, lies in the acceptance of the historical facts about Australian nation-building, the inclusion of Indigenous people in the nation-building process to counter previous exclusion and the development of a relationship between Indigenous and non-Indigenous Australians that in part takes the form of formal structures and institutions.

A preamble to the Constitution

Although the creation of a preamble falls under the category of constitutional change, it can also be seen as an important form of symbolic recognition.

The Constitution is Australia's foundational document. It sets up its system of governance. For this reason, it is appropriate that it

---

6   *Mabo v Queensland (No 2)* (1992) 175 CLR 1.
7   For an elaboration of this argument, see Henry Reynolds, 1996, *Aboriginal Sovereignty: Three Nations, One Australia,* Allen & Unwin.

have a preamble that reflects Australia's societal values and that the values expressed in that preamble should express the spirit, beliefs, aspirations, hopes and ideologies of the nation. The purpose of a preamble to an Act is to give context to the legislation. It has been accepted in the common law and in legislation that the preamble can provide guidance to interpretation when sections of the Act are not clear.[8] The preamble can therefore offer clarification if legislation is unclear in purpose or intent and/or provide guidance to interpretation. For this reason, it is important that any amendment be given full weight as a preamble.[9]

In November 1999, in conjunction with a referendum question about whether to alter the Constitution to replace the Governor-General as the Head of State,[10] a question was also put to the Australian public that proposed a new Preamble to the Constitution. The drafting was not done with bi-partisan support or community consultation, but rather combined the literary talents of poet Les Murray and Prime Minister John Howard. It's reference to Indigenous people was as follows:

> Since time immemorial our land has been inhabited by Aborigines and Torres Strait Islanders, who are honoured for their ancient and continuing cultures.[11]

There was widespread criticism of many components of the Murray-Howard preamble. The draft was rewritten, and after consultation with the Australian Democrats, the preamble put to the Australian public at the referendum included the amended clause:

> honouring Aborigines and Torres Strait Islanders, the nation's first people, for their deep kinship with their lands and for their ancient and continuing cultures which enrich the life of our country ...[12]

---

8   *Bowtell v Goldsbrough, Mort and Co Ltd* (1905) 3 CLR 444; *Wacando v Commonwealth and Queensland* (1981) 148 CLR 1.
9   The preamble proposed at the 1999 Constitutional Referendum was not going to be given interpretive weight if it were enacted. Any preamble that recognised Indigenous people, history, culture and rights must be given full interpretive value as a preamble or its ability to influence rights protection will be erased.
10 T Blackshield and G Williams, 2002, *Australian Constitutional Law and theory, Commentary and Materials,* 3rd edn, Federation Press, p 1326.
11 Ibid, p 1330.
12 Ibid, p 1331.

Neither the original nor amended clause gave recognition to the rights, laws, distinct histories or sovereignty of Indigenous people.

The preamble as proposed was also problematic because it would have inserted a new clause in the Constitution that prevented the preamble from having any interpretive value. The result would have been a preamble that did not properly represent the unique place Indigenous people have within Australian society and it would have been an instrument that shed no light on the grey areas of the Constitution.

Australians voted resoundingly to reject the inclusion of the proposed preamble. (They also rejected the proposed plan to replace the Governor-General as Head of State.)

It is important to note here that when the Constitution was drafted, it was not only instituted with the belief that Indigenous people were a dying race, it also was written with the assumption that Australia would continue its anti-Asian, White Australia immigration policy.[13] A new preamble that would emphasise diversity, tolerance and a new relationship between the different cultures within Australia would better reflect a vision of Australia that is shared by Indigenous and non-Indigenous people — and the reality of the nation today.

The suggestion of including a preamble to the Constitution is less contentious than the issue of the subject matter of such a preamble. There are many facets of Australian society that are valued — multiculturalism, equality — and that may be appropriate to include in a preamble to the Constitution to embody the 'spirit of our nation'. With Australia's history, it is fitting that a preamble to the Constitution enshrine an acknowledgment that Indigenous people were the original custodians of the land. Post-*Mabo*, it is not controversial of itself to acknowledge the prior occupation/presence in Australia of Indigenous people. Overturning the doctrine of *terra nullius* merely confirmed a fact that existed independently of legal doctrine, that Australia's Indigenous people occupied Australia before the British arrived.

It would also seem that the recognition of a new relationship between Indigenous and non-Indigenous nations in a preamble to the Constitution would be an effective way of enshrining this concept of nation-building. This belated nation-building allows inclusion while recognising uniqueness.

---

13   G Williams, 2002, *Human Rights Under the Australian Constitution*, Oxford University Press. See generally Chapter 2, 'Human rights and the drafting of the Australian Constitution'.

To provide a base for interpretation that could facilitate improved rights protection, a constitutional preamble should provide:
- a symbolic recognition of sovereignty and prior occupation and ownership;
- a redefinition of the relationship that Indigenous people have with Australia; and
- the granting of better rights protection.

It should contain reference to the following:
- Indigenous people as the original owners of Australia;
- the dispossession and dispersal Indigenous people suffered upon exclusion from their traditional lands by the authority of the Crown;
- the distinct cultural status of Indigenous people, whose traditional laws, customs and ways of life have evolved over thousands of years;
- a collective recognition of Indigenous people as a distinct people, including protection of traditional cultures, lifestyles, and Indigenous rights;
- rights of self-government for Indigenous people within the nation-state; and
- rights of Indigenous people to lands, resources and their benefits as a base for self-sufficiency and development of Indigenous communities and families, including protection of existing economic resources (eg, fishing and hunting territories).

This might seem like a merely symbolic gesture. But it may give rise to something more substantial. Since a preamble is contextual, it will not necessarily be used in the interpretation of the Act itself but it can be invoked to clear up any uncertainty in the body of the document. In this way, what may seem like a merely symbolic gesture could provide a balance in the interpretation of rights — and their *bona fide* protection under the Constitution will undo or counter racism entrenched in the Constitution when the document was drafted.

Symbolic recognition that could alter the way Australians see their history will also affect their views on the kind of society they would like to become. It would alter the symbols and sentiments Australians use to express their identity and ideals. It would change the context in which debates about Indigenous issues and rights take place. It would alter the way the relationship between Indigenous and non-Indigenous Australians is conceptualised. These shifts will affect the way Australians want their institutions, like the Constitution, to work and will begin to permeate them. In this way, the long-term effects of symbolic recognition could be quite substantial.

Towards Constitutional change

A Legislative Bill of Rights

Distress over the outcome of the case brought by Lorna Cabillo and Peter Gunner seems to have eclipsed the findings of the High Court in the 1997 *Stolen Generations* case of *Kruger v Commonwealth*,[14] (see p 28). While Cabillo and Gunner sought to find responsibility and recompense for their removal and treatment under state care primarily in the principles of tort law, the plaintiffs in *Kruger* based their claims on various explicit or implied rights in the Australian Constitution including the implied freedom of movement, the right to the freedom of religion and an implied right to legal equality.

The failure of the plaintiffs in the *Kruger* case starkly highlights the void of rights protection in the Australian Constitution and shows that, even where rights might be specifically protected, they are not easily invoked. The *Stolen Generations* case is just one instance of experiences that heighten profound injustice against Indigenous Australians. The same systematic deprivation of rights protection occurs in relation to the erosion of native title rights and treatment under the criminal justice system.

The result of the 1999 Republic and Preamble Referendum shows the problem for constitutional protection of specific rights for Indigenous people. The Australian electorate is traditionally resistant to constitutional amendments, rarely voting to pass them, and Indigenous rights are a politically contentious matter that would have trouble gaining the broad support needed. While constitutional protection of these rights is the most desirable and the best possible protection of Indigenous rights in Australia, it is politically unachievable, at least in the short term, and remains a long-term goal.

A Bill of Rights is not the answer to the plethora of problems facing Indigenous people but it should be supported as a solid and profound first step towards improved rights protection. A first step in working towards constitutional protection would be a Bill of Rights in legislative form, as has been adopted in New Zealand and the United Kingdom. Not only does this have the advantage of being a

---

14   *Kruger v Commonwealth* (1997) 190 CLR 1.

minimalist approach, it also has the added attraction of being a process that could engage the public in the content of the bill, giving Australians a greater interest and feeling of association with and ownership of the outcome.[15] This would help to create a culture of rights protection in the Australian psyche and perhaps help to shift some popular misconceptions about Indigenous rights, providing a basis upon which stronger protections could be built.

A legislative Bill of Rights existed for two decades before becoming entrenched in the Canadian Constitution. The effect of the inclusion of a Bill of Rights into the Canadian legal system means that all Canadian citizens now see themselves as rights-holding entities and the dialogue of rights between Indigenous and non-Indigenous Canadians is in a shared language.

The content of a Bill of Rights is as contentious as the idea of whether or not Australia should have one. Ideas for appropriate content could be found in existing statements of self-determination. The following clause is taken from the Barunga statement.

> (in accordance with the Universal Declaration on Human Rights, the International Covenant on Economic, Social, and Cultural Rights, the International Covenant on Civil and Political Rights, and the Convention for the Elimination of all forms of Racial Discrimination) rights to life, liberty, security of person, food, clothing, housing, medical care, education and employment opportunities, necessary social services and other basic rights.

This clause acknowledges that international human rights instruments may provide some guide to the content of Indigenous rights protection. That being so, international human rights instruments may be a starting point for the content of a Bill of Rights. The substance of the International Covenant on Civil and Political Rights (ICCPR) would offer a guide to some of the rights appropriate for inclusion in a Bill of Rights. The ICCPR contains the following:

- Right to life (Art 6)
- Right to liberty and security of person (Art 9)
- Right to freedom of movement (Art 12)
- Right to due process before the courts (Art 14)
- Rights to privacy (Art 17)

---

15 This has been emphasised by George Williams in his book *A Bill of Rights for Australia* (University of New South Wales Press, 2000).

- Right to freedom of thought, conscience and religion (Art 18)
- Right to freedom of expression (Art 19)
- Right of peaceful assembly (Art 21)
- Right to freedom of association (Art 22)
- Equality before the law (Art 26)
- Minority rights to participate in their own culture, practice their own religion and use their own language (Art 27)

We can see some of the same rights that the plaintiffs in *Kruger* claimed were violated by the policy of removing Indigenous children. The principles of the CERD and the principles of the Convention on the Elimination of all forms of Discrimination Against Women (CEDAW) should also be considered for inclusion.

The International Covenant on Economic, Social and Cultural Rights (ICESCR) should also be considered for inclusion but it must be remembered that, unlike the ICCPR, the ICESCR contains references to economic and cultural rights rather than recognised civil and political rights. Inclusion of its subject matter into a domestic Bill will be more contentious because the rights it recognises (such as those listed below) are harder to define and quantify:

- Right to work (Art 6)
- Enjoyment of just and favorable conditions of work (Art 7)
- Right to form trade unions (Art 8)
- Right to social security (Art 9)
- Right to an adequate standard of living (Art 11)
- Right to the highest attainable standard of physical and mental health (Art 12)
- Right to education (Art 13)

One approach to be considered is to treat the contents of the ICCPR, CERD and CEDAW as 'core' rights and the substance of the ICESCR as rights to be considered in the interpretation of those core rights. This approach recognises that some individual rights can only be protected by mechanisms that protect the community or a minority group as a whole. For instance, the right to enjoy one's culture may vest in the individual but is empty in substance unless some recognition is given to the communal aspect of that individual right.

Even if a Bill of Rights did not deal with specific Indigenous claims, it is easy to see how Indigenous people would be assisted by the content of a Bill of Rights that resonated with rights already recognised as fundamental under international law.

Apart from general provisions in a Bill of Rights that would apply to Indigenous people, there may also be specific recognition of rights that have some special importance to Indigenous people in light of historical experience. Such a provision may look something like this:

(1) In addition to the rights included in this legislation, Indigenous people are recognised as having the right to:
   (a) substantive equality in the appreciation of rights;
   (b) non-discrimination in relation to the provision of goods and services by the government or where public services are provided by private enterprise;
   (c) the same level of service delivery by the government or where public services are provided by private enterprise as enjoyed by other members of the community in relation to housing, education and health;
   (d) due process and protection of the laws;
   (e) enjoy their native title entitlements;
   (f) protection of their recognised property interests;
   (g) rights of land management recognised under land rights legislation;
   (h) protection of rights provided under cultural heritage legislation;
   (i) increased self-government through regional framework agreements;
(2) Indigenous people have the right to be consulted and to participate in decision-making processes that will affect their rights which are protected under this legislation.

Rather than articulating specific rights, a Bill of Rights could contain a general provision recognising Indigenous rights. Such a provision might read:

> All rights contained within the Bill of Rights extend to Indigenous people in a way that will achieve substantive equality.

A general approach has the advantage of being broad and aspirational and will allow, in a legislative Bill of Rights, for the development of the specifics of the extent of that right over time. However, its lack of definition may make its inclusion politically contentious.

Most important for the protection of the rights of Indigenous people is the inclusion within a legislative Bill of Rights of an 'equality' or 'non-discrimination' clause. However, if such a clause is included, the legislation must offer clear guidelines on how that provision should be interpreted. To avoid the further entrenchment of systemic racism under the guise of 'equal application of law', direction needs to be given on the goal of a legislative Bill of Rights that would inform interpretation of its provisions. Emphasis must be placed on the *achievement of equality as a result* of the application of rules, not just in the process of applying them. This means that the Bill of Rights must have a goal of achieving substantive rather than formal equality.

A legislative Bill of Rights offering protection of fundamental human rights should be of overriding importance and should not be derogated from easily. If it is simple for the legislature to side-step the provisions of such legislation, it would give the impression that the Bill of Rights was merely symbolic. Yet mechanisms must remain in place to ensure that, in extreme instances where anomalies in interpretation have given rise to undesired effects, the legislation can be amended to achieve its intended results. This may be done, for instance, by allowing the legislative Bill of Rights to be overridden only when the intention is explicitly stated in other legislation or the derogation is approved by Parliament through a special procedure such as by allowing it to be overridden only by a two-thirds majority in both houses.

Increased protection of rights recognised under international law

With no protection of Indigenous rights within the Australian legal system, it is not surprising that Indigenous people would increasingly rely on the arena in which standards of human rights have been developed: international human rights instruments and law. This has already been shown by reference to those standards in Indigenous expressions of self-determination such as the Barunga statement.

There are three aspects to the connection between international law and Indigenous rights that can provide starting points to improved rights protection in Australian law:

- compliance with obligations under ratified international human rights instruments;
- increased incorporation of ratified human rights instruments in domestic legislation; and
- continued participation by Indigenous people in the international arena.

Compliance with obligations under ratified international human rights instruments

On 24 March 2000, the CERD Committee issued a report critical of the Howard Government's record on human rights protected under CERD. In particular, the concluding observations by the Committee included the following expressions of concern:

- the absence of an entrenched provision to ensure protection from racial discrimination;
- provisions of the *Native Title Amendment Act* 1998 (Cth) which could reduce further the protection of the rights of native title holders;
- the Commonwealth Government's failure to support a formal national apology and its position that the provision of monetary compensation for those forcibly and unjustifiably separated from their families is inappropriate on the basis that such practices were intended to 'assist the people whom they affected';[16]
- the mandatory sentencing schemes that target offences committed disproportionately by Indigenous Australians, especially juveniles, creating a racially discriminatory impact on already high rates of Indigenous incarceration; and
- the extent of the continuing discrimination faced by Indigenous Australians in the enjoyment of their economic, social and cultural rights.[17]

The CERD report drew attention to the wide range of issues that are of concern to Indigenous communities at the present time.

From reconciliation to penal provisions, it covered the spectrum of matters that illustrate inherent discrimination in Australian laws and government institutions (including legislative indifference and judicial complicity) that contribute to the continuing and profound socio-economic disparity between Indigenous and non-Indigenous Australians.

Although the report was in no way erroneous, the government condemned CERD, claiming that it gave too much emphasis to non-governmental submissions and took a 'blatantly political and partisan

---

16 CERD/C/56/Misc42/Rev3, 24 March 2000, para 13.
17 Ibid, para 18.

approach' that 'ignored the significant progress made in Australia across the spectrum of Indigenous policies.'[18]

This view that the CERD report was based on 'uncritical acceptance of the claims of domestic political lobbies' led the government to establish a review of the operation of the UN treaty committee system as it affects Australia.[19]

This attitude towards the monitoring of Australia's human rights record invites the comment that the Australian government views compliance mechanisms as an unwelcome, biased interference with its domestic affairs and implies that Australia is better placed to interpret and assess its track record on human rights than any outside body. This policy position taken by the government was further entrenched as a response to similar critical reports on performance of Australia's obligations under the ICCPR and ICESCR.

On 29 August 2000, a joint press release was issued by the Minister for Foreign Affairs, the Attorney-General and the Minister for Immigration and Multicultural Affairs.[20] It announced that Australia was seeking to improve the effectiveness of the UN committee system by insisting on reforms.

In particular, it sought to ensure 'adequate recognition of the primary role of democratically elected governments and the subordinate role of Non-Government Organisations (NGOs).'

This would lessen the role played in the international arena by organisations such as Amnesty International and ATSIC. The press release also announced that 'Cabinet decided Australia's strategic engagement with the treaty committee system should be dependent on the extent to which effective reform occurs.'

This policy will see a more 'economical and selective approach' to participation with treaty committees. Further, 'Australia will only agree to visits to Australia by treaty committees and requests from the Committee on Human Rights 'mechanisms' for visits and the provision of information where there is a compelling reason to do so.'

---

18   Press release, Minister for Foreign Affairs, Alexander Downer, 30 March 2000.

19   Press release, Minister for Foreign Affairs, Alexander Downer, 30 March 2000.

20   Joint Press Release issued by Minister for Foreign Affairs (Alexander Downer), Attorney-General (The Hon Daryl Williams AM QC MP), Minister for Immigration and Multicultural Affairs (The Hon Philip Ruddock MP), Joint media release, Tuesday, 29 August 2000, FA97.

There are three points to make about this approach taken by the Australian government towards the monitoring of its human rights record:

- the irony of Australia's claim to be the best arbiter of its domestic rights situation when it has so few mechanisms within its legal system to ensure that rights are recognised and protected;
- the irony of the complaint of the Australian government, which led the international community into East Timor to prevent human rights abuses, about the monitoring of its own record by that very same international community; and
- the parallel that can be drawn between the Australian government's attempt to silence Indigenous people at the international level when they seek to assert their recognised rights and the continual attempt by the same government to erode rights to negotiate and to consult by rights-holders in relation to activities that will extinguish native title.

Australia must reconsider this direction in policy and remain faithful to its obligations to participate in the UN committee processes, particularly until there are improved domestic mechanisms in place that provide strengthened rights protection.

Increased incorporation of ratified human rights instruments in domestic legislation

Many of the protections sought by Indigenous people in Australia under the claim to sovereignty and exercise of self-determination are recognised by international human rights instruments. The federal government has the ability, under the external affairs power embodied in s 51(xxix) of the Constitution, to implement legislation that will put into force the rights and principles in any international convention ratified by Australia. There are several legislative examples of the federal government attempting to implement its obligations under international law. After signing and ratifying the ICCPR and CERD, the Human Rights Commission and Equal Opportunity Commission and State Anti-Discrimination Boards were established to receive complaints about violations of rights and discriminatory practices.

Even though the status of international standards under Australian law in the absence of implementing legislation is uncertain, the High Court has exhibited a willingness to infer those standards into domestic law. For example, in *Teoh v Minister for Immigration*,[21] members of the High Court referred to rights of children under an international convention ratified by the Australian government, indicating that the judiciary would actively interpret rights that Australia had assented to.[22] This acknowledgment was ambiguous since the same principle relied upon in the international treaty, namely, 'the best interest of the child' was also included in Australian legislation, the *Family Law Act* 1975 (Cth).[23] While it is unclear whether the court's decision in the *Teoh* case was based solely on the international convention or was supportable by Australian law, it is of note that the judiciary would look to Australia's international obligations to secure rights and thus elevate the importance of international human rights instruments within Australian jurisprudence. Also of note was the reaction to the court's decision in that case. There was strong resistance from conservative sectors of the community to the idea that rights could be developed by an active judiciary rather than by Parliament, but to date no legislation nor constitutional amendment has occurred to diminish the court's activism. However, the less enthusiastic attitudes towards judicial activism and implied rights of the more recent appointments to the bench may curtail it.

This active incorporation of international standards is a far more satisfactory approach than relying on the judiciary to imply those rights. It could be achieved by the legislature taking a more active role in incorporating those international rights and principles to facilitate the filtration of international human rights norms into domestic Australian law. One way this could be done is to note relevant international human rights instruments in appropriate legislation. Section 15AB(2)(d) of the *Acts Interpretation Act* 1901 (Cth) allows for the reference to 'any treaty or other international agreement that is referred to in the Act' to be used as interpretive material to confirm the meaning of legislation or to resolve an ambiguity, obscurity or

---

21 (1995) 128 ALR 353.
22 Other implied rights have been found in the Constitution: freedom of political communication – *Nationwide News Pty Ltd v Wills* (1992) 177 CLR 1; *Australian Capital Television Pty Ltd v Commonwealth* (1992) 177 CLR 106; *Theophanous v Herald & Weekly Times Ltd* (1994) 182 CLR 104; freedom of movement and association – *Lange v Australian Broadcasting Corporation* (1997) 145 ALR 96; *Kruger v Commonwealth* (1997) 146 ALR 126; implied right to due process – *Leeth v Commonwealth* (1992) 174 CLR 455.
23 *Family Law Act* 1975 (Cth), s 67ZC, Orders relating to the welfare of children.

absurdity.[24] This active referencing and incorporation of international human rights standards allows for a stronger basis of rights protection than reliance upon judicial inference.

Continued participation by Indigenous people in the international arena

Indigenous people have begun to leave a mark on the institutions of the UN, primarily through the activities of the Working Group on Indigenous Peoples. In 1994, the Commission on Human Rights Sub-Commission on the Prevention of Discrimination Against Minorities recommended to the Economic and Social Council (ECOSOC) that it approve the participation of Indigenous persons and organisations, without regard to consultative status, in meetings of the UN, including the Commission itself, at which the Draft Declaration on Indigenous Peoples was being discussed.[25] This effectively opened up the forum to Indigenous groups and individuals from around the world without requiring them to seek consultative status first. It was one of the first steps towards allowing consultation with and input from groups whose members would be the direct beneficiaries of the resultant international document. It was also an important precedent to allowing greater participation by non-state entities in the international arena.

Access to the UN through the Working Group on Indigenous Peoples also had a profound affect on the Australian Indigenous people who participated in the forum. Mick Dodson, then ATSISJC Commissioner, explained the impact attending the session had on him:

> [W]e had gathered there united by our shared frustration with the dominant systems in our own countries and their consistent failure to deliver justice. It was the beginning of my personal identification as one of the world's Indigenous peoples. We were all looking for, and demanding, justice from a higher authority.[26]

Dodson pointed to three consequences that the open forum developed.

---

24 As per s 15AB(1).
25 UN Doc E/CN4/Sub2/1994/L60, 24 August 1994.
26 M Dodson, 1995, Aboriginal and Torres Strait Islander Social Justice Commission, *Introductory Remarks*, United Nations Procedures and Indigenous Australians, Sydney, 28 June.

- It provided a meeting place for Indigenous peoples to meet with and discuss issues with other Indigenous peoples. This allowed for information exchange and network building that has strengthened Indigenous rights movements around the world.
- The ability to raise grievances outside of the rhetoric of election campaigns and vote winning tactics in the domestic arena, however lowly the forum within the UN framework, allows Indigenous peoples to make claims and accusations against violating states. It is an opportunity that Indigenous peoples in Australia have open to them when constantly frustrated about the way their issues are politicised and trivialised in Australia.
- Participation in the international structures gives confidence to indigenous peoples who claim that their rights have been violated. Their assertions are reinforced by the existence of human rights instruments that articulate the legitimacy of the claims that they are making. This adds to the veracity with which these claims can be asserted against the state.[27]

The Draft Declaration on the Rights of Indigenous Peoples has been the major achievement of the Working Group on Indigenous Peoples.[28] As the document stands, it reflects the aspirations of Indigenous peoples. This principled approach could be reached because Member States dropped out of the drafting process, allowing the document to reflect the agenda of Indigenous peoples in a way no other UN document has. The tone of the document was achieved because it was the result of consensus between Indigenous peoples with a shared history of surviving colonisation rather than the result of consensus to accommodate the agenda of Member States. Although international mechanisms and norms are not always responsive or effective, the activity of Indigenous advocates within the frameworks of the UN and international law highlights the inventiveness of Indigenous peoples in pursuing alternative approaches towards better rights protections. In addition to providing evidence of energetic agency, this experience shows how small changes within a structured framework can facilitate larger institutional and normative changes.

However, it is important to remember that the Declaration has a long path to travel through the UN system before it is presented to

---

27 M Dodson, 1995, Aboriginal and Torres Strait Islander Social Justice Commission, *Introductory Remarks*, United Nations Procedures and Indigenous Australians, Sydney, 28 June.
28 UN Doc E/CN4/Sub21993/29/Annex I, 23 August 1993.

States to sign and ratify. The aspirational approach contained within the Draft Declaration is unlikely to remain once the document is reviewed through the UN processes. Throughout these subsequent stages, Indigenous peoples will have less, if any, input into the development of the document. It may have been hoped that the Declaration would create a formal international legal declaration on Indigenous rights that would enhance the protection of the rights of Indigenous peoples and reinforce their status as international legal entities. Member States have already shown that they will be reluctant to adopt a document that ties them to the aspirations contained in the current Draft. In the end, it is the Member States who will decide the substantive content of the Declaration. When, and if, adopted by the UN General Assembly, the Declaration will not be legally binding and there will be no obligation to legislate in each Member State (such as Australia) until the Member State ratifies it. So despite the aspirational content of the Draft Declaration, the limitations of its usefulness in the long term are beginning to become apparent and it may be the right time to reflect on other avenues of monitoring and redress within the UN system.

Much emphasis has been placed on the Draft Declaration at the expense of other, already ratified international human rights instruments that provide recognition of rights such as:

- Universal Declaration of Human Rights (UDHR)
- International Covenant on Civil and Political Rights (ICCPR)
- International Covenant on Economic, Social and Cultural Rights (ICESCR)
- Convention to Eliminate all forms of Racial Discrimination (CERD)
- Convention on the Elimination of all forms of Discrimination Against Women (CEDAW)

These instruments set out broad declarations of international human rights and their provisions cover the areas specified by Indigenous peoples as being of relevance, including:

- cultural protection (language, heritage, religious practices);
- recognition of land claims (though not access to natural resources); and
- a range of individual rights (non-discrimination, education, social services, health services and basic civil and political rights).

It would be wrong to give the impression that the UN institutions and international human rights instruments adequately meet and protect the needs of Indigenous peoples but they *do* provide avenues for raising issues within the framework of these instruments. Indigenous groups have been actively working within the institutions of the UN to ensure their experience is noted by monitoring bodies whenever relevant. Many international covenants have complaint, monitoring and reporting procedures and Indigenous peoples have been effective at using these processes to highlight breaches of human rights due to government policy and action. In addition, this participation is a way of ensuring a change in the longer term as they become norms under international law; these are norms that develop through the establishment of accepted principles, such as non-discrimination on the basis of race, in the international human rights framework. These emerging international customary laws impact on all countries, even those who have not ratified international treaties and conventions, because the emerging standards of the majority are used to measure the performance of the rest.

Indigenous peoples themselves understand how the international arena can provide a springboard for substantive changes that will allow the greater respect for the rights of Indigenous peoples within their own states. The continual involvement of Indigenous peoples in this arena is important because of the contribution made to the development of international norms, the perspective provided to monitoring bodies and because of the experience that advocacy in the international arena gives those Indigenous peoples who attend.

Constitutional protection

The introduction of a legislative Bill of Rights and the increased incorporation of international human rights standards into Australia's domestic laws would create an increased awareness of rights amongst Australian citizens and also an increased awareness of themselves as rights-holding entities. It would allow people to articulate claims and harms in a shared vocabulary of rights. This culture of increased awareness of and dialogue about rights is needed before there can be consensus and support to enable certain core rights and principles to be entrenched in the Australian Constitution.

The constitutional changes that have been mooted to date includes changes to the existing document and the insertion of new clauses. Recurring suggestions for constitutional change that would improve the ability to protect Indigenous rights include the following.

Repeal Section 25

Section 25 of the Constitution contains the following:

> if by the law of any State all persons of any races are disqualified from voting at elections ...

The racist implications of the section offend principles of racial equality and even though it may be unlikely that the states will pass such legislation, Australia needs to move away from expressions of such overt racism in the text of the Constitution.

A new preamble to the Constitution

A preamble is important because it sets the tone for the rest of the document. It can be used to give assistance in interpreting the Act that follows. Particularly in the Australian Constitution, a new preamble will offer an opportunity to articulate Australians' shared goals, principles and ideals. If recognition of prior sovereignty and prior ownership were contained in a preamble, courts may be able to read the Constitution as clearly promoting Indigenous rights protection, clearing up the question left unanswered by the *Hindmarsh Island Bridge* case.[29]

A Bill of Rights

As the *Kruger* case showed, very few rights are protected by the Australian Constitution.[30] Those that appear in the document have been interpreted in a minimal manner. Although members of the High Court have held that there are implied rights, this is a precarious approach to rights protection. A Bill of Rights that granted rights and freedoms to everyone would be a non-contentious way in which to ensure some Indigenous rights protection. Public discussion needs to be focused on whether Australia should have a constitutional or a legislative Bill of Rights. A legislative Bill of Rights could be viewed as an interim step towards a constitutionally entrenched Bill of Rights.[31]

---

29 *Kartinyeri v Commonwealth* (1998) 195 CLR 337.
30 *Kruger v Commonwealth* (1997) 190 CLR 1.
31 For a full discussion of the legislative Bill of Rights model, see Williams 2000.

A non-discrimination clause

Such a clause could enshrine the notion of non-discrimination in the Constitution. Such a clause must also adhere to the principle that affirmative action mechanisms aid in the achievement of non-discrimination.

Specific constitutional protection

An amendment could be made to the Constitution include a specific provision to protect Indigenous rights. In Canada, a comparable jurisdiction with a comparable history and comparable relationship with its Indigenous communities, the Canadian *Constitutional Act* 1982 added the following provision to the Constitution.

> Section 35(1): the existing aboriginal and treaty rights of the aboriginal peoples of Canada are hereby recognised and affirmed.

The link between these constitutional changes and the past failure to protect Indigenous rights become apparent. In this way, calls for changes to the existing constitutional framework can be interpreted as an assertion that the Constitution, in its current form, does not protect the rights of those who suffer from systemic and institutionalised racism.

Towards regional autonomy

One of the strongest themes running through claims for recognition of sovereignty and the exercise of self-determination is that initiatives need to have a strong local and regional community focus. This emphasis is hardly surprising, given that the best way to ensure effective representation is to make political units smaller and more community-based. Involvement with organisations at this level can generate a feeling of consensus and inclusiveness that membership of large political parties and systems are unable to provide.

Delegation of decision-making power to smaller political units would allow the breakdown of large councils and shires into smaller neighbourhood groups that can more effectively pinpoint and address community needs.

These smaller political units become more responsive; they allow for more active participation from interested community members who feel alienated from large-scale political institutions.

This community-based focus also would enable Indigenous community groups to take responsibility for decision-making processes on issues that affect them. Such groups should be active in the areas of cultural protection, health, and education. This moves from a model for decision-making processes that see government departments making decisions and developing policies that then filter down to Indigenous communities to a model that embraces a bottom-up approach to policy-making. (See figure opposite.)

There are already some practical examples and theoretical formulations of this grass-roots approach to increased Indigenous decision-making.

The Ngaanyatjarra Aboriginal community

In an agreement between the WA government and the Ngaanyatjarra Aboriginal community, a land transfer of the freehold title of 25 million hectares of land was made to the Indigenous community of about 1600 members. Upon transfer, the area, which was heralded as almost amounting 'to the creation of a Ngaanyatjarra State',[32] became a shire of WA.

The willing participation of the WA government, which had long been resistant to land claims and other Indigenous rights, is possibly related to the fact that the agreement expresses a commitment to developing mines in the area, including prospecting for uranium.

Yet the arrangement allowed for the economic independence of a once impoverished community with a plethora of social problems: petrol sniffing, high rates of violence, alcoholism. The community now has well-run business interests and is concentrating on developing a cultural centre to celebrate the art produced by community members. These arrangements that suit remote, geographically distinct groups – if there is a land base and a population large enough to support the arrangements – do not represent all Indigenous communities.[33]

---

32 This is the characterisation made by the *Sydney Morning Herald* ('Historic 'State' for Aborigines', 16 November 1996, p 1). It is somewhat sensationalised.

33 The Pitjantjnatjara in South Australia would be one of the few groups that immediately seems to fit the criteria, occupying a large land base and having a distinctive culture which includes traditional practices of dispute resolution and law.

TOWARDS IMPROVED RIGHTS PROTECTION

CURRENT SITUATION
A top-down approach

**Government Department
Aboriginal Unit**
decides policy (often through a consultation process)

Community
recipient of services

DISPERSAL OF POWER
A bottom-up approach

State Government Body
co-ordinate regional groups,
administer funding and provide support

Regional Bodies
co-ordinate local community groups
administer funding and provide support

Local Communities
decision-making power

Noel Pearson's Cape York 'Interface'

Noel Pearson has spoken of establishing 'a new interface between the outside structures of government, the Queensland government, the Commonwealth government and the Aboriginal and Torres Strait Islander Commission and the Cape York community.'[34] This 'interface' then becomes a

> meeting place between the state and the Cape York community and its leaders. All government programs and inputs into Cape York need to be negotiated through this interface. The state would negotiate with Aboriginal community representatives at this interface, design programs and develop co-operative agreements on how these programs will be delivered on the ground.[35]

Pearson's model hands decision-making power back to the community. As he notes:

> Given the opportunity, the community can devise imaginative and enterprising ideas that give expression to the reciprocity principle. It is the community and its leaders who need to develop strategies for the development of their community. It is the community that needs to develop ideas that address the educational, health, and recreational needs of their people, so that individuals are empowered and engaged in the solution of their own problems and those of their families and communities.[36]

This vision sees a new role for the state, one of junior partner, relinquishing the role of sole service provider, especially in relation to social policy. Pearson sees this 'regional interface' devolving responsibility to Indigenous communities which, in turn, will need to devolve responsibility to families and individuals. The state's role is to secure the necessary resources.

> Of course, the critical ingredient will be the provision of resources by the state. When we say that negative welfare is destructive, we mean that it needs to be changed, not that the resources should be denied or diminished.[37]

---

34 Pearson, 2000, p 170.
35 Pearson, 2000, p 171.
36 Pearson, 2000, p 172.
37 Pearson, 2000, p 174.

Local government control

Darryl Pearce, CEO of the South Western Aboriginal Land and Sea Council, has noted that:

> [w]ith control of local government, Aboriginal people can control water, sewerage, roads, etc — all the municipal services ... With control of local government in place, Aboriginal people can work towards self-government on a greater scale.[38]

He goes on to say:

> what Aboriginal people are talking about are better ways of delivering health and education policies which most affect us. We are talking about doing these things in a way which suits Aboriginal people. We are talking about having control of the funds which are rightfully ours, for the carrying out of these functions and using them as we see fit.[39]

Like Pearson, Pearce is seeking a way to break out of the cycle of welfare dependency and, from a sound economic base, achieve self-government. Similar to the Ngaanyatjarra experience, he has identified local government as an appropriate level for the exercise of this greater community control.

The model of the local council is a useful one, as it is a regulatory entity that covers a distinct territory that also falls under the jurisdiction of State and federal powers but allows the community the power to make regulations and set up institutions:

- Indigenous communities are no different from other communities in Australia that can be subject to special laws and regulations. In this way, there can be no difference between allowing a municipal council the authority to make by-laws for people who live in their district and Local Land Councils creating by-laws that regulate the conduct of people living on areas of land owned and administered by a Land Council.

- Powers could be delegated from the State or federal government that allow Indigenous communities to establish institutions and infrastructure that would allow greater community autonomy.

---

38 D Pearce, 'Aboriginal Self Government', in C Fletcher (ed), *Aboriginal Self-Determination in Australia*, Australian Institute of Aboriginal and Torres Strait Islander Studies, 1994, p 48.
39 Pearce, 1994, p 48.

- State legislation would need to be passed that would enable the establishment of Indigenous administered schools, health services and courts that dealt with matters formally the domain of the State.
- Federal government can make legislation under the race power[40] to delegate powers formally held by the federal government. Those powers include matters under the jurisdiction of the federal courts, importantly including family law matters (including custody and adoption).

Local decision-making models

Urban communities can develop models of decentralised decision and policy-making which can empower communities at a grass-roots level, allowing the concerns of the Indigenous community to be represented. Such models can facilitate active participation in political and governmental practices at a level at which an individual can feel that his or her opinion can make a difference. This concentration of decision-making processes will allow communities to target their needs more specifically, avoiding the problems that can occur when decision-making occurs at a higher level and misses some of the subtle, and some not so subtle, differences between different Indigenous communities. Aboriginal Education Consultative Groups provide an example of such a proposed grass-roots model that operates successfully in the urban community. They have a branch in each area where members of the community interact with schools and provide advice about teaching Indigenous perspectives and also provide Indigenous teaching aides. This participation in the schooling of Indigenous children has several advantages:

- It creates an opportunity for members of the community to participate actively in the institutions of the community.
- It injects diversity into the school system through the generation of different cultural perspectives that will influence programs and policies as a result of the participation of people from different cultural groups.
- It allows for the development of programs that meet the needs of specific communities.

---

40 Section 51(xxvi) of the Constitution allows the federal government the power to legislate in relation to matters concerning race. This power has been invoked to pass legislation concerning Indigenous people such as the *Aboriginal and Torres Strait Islander Commission Act* 1988 (Cth).

Indigenous communities are seeking more autonomy and are increasingly showing interest in developing community-based programs such as community courts, community policing and Indigenous schools. Some of these programs have been the initiative of community members but this grass-roots approach to decision-making could be facilitated by a formal delegation of powers from the State and federal governments.

At a federal level, claims for greater autonomy within Indigenous communities would require a delegation of authority from federal, State and local governments. Provisions for such agreements could be made with the federal government through legislative provisions enacted through the race power of s 51(xxvi) of the Constitution. At a State level, it would seem that the powers of Indigenous communities could be developed on the local council model and/or through the facilitation of community-based groups such as the Aboriginal Education Consultative Group.

Such judicial and administrative powers can be layered, co-existing with and complementing federal and State jurisdiction. This complementary role counters assertions that the increased autonomy of Indigenous communities undermines State and national sovereignty or is unworkable in practice.

However, there is one note of caution about a process of delegation of power that would focus mainly on the reproduction of institutions of the dominant culture into Indigenous communities. There is a tendency to merely mirror the institutions of the dominant culture without thinking about whether they work for Indigenous people and without consideration of modifications or alternatives. The plan of introducing new institutional arrangements into communities is usually to place the set of institutions used in the dominant culture into the minority culture, perhaps scaled down and with some tinkering done to make them more 'culturally specific'. This uncritical 'mirroring' of institutions in Indigenous communities may erode traditional cultural values and practices. These transplanted institutional structures erode the cultural differences of the Indigenous community and stifle an environment where institutional experimentation can be rich. This phenomena occurs at many levels: constitutions, tribal courts, mediation processes.

Patrick Sullivan's[41] work in the Kimberley region has led him to conclude that 'formulating and implementing regional plans involves

---

41 Visiting Research Fellow at the Australian Institute of Aboriginal and Torres Strait Islander Studies.

Aborigines taking control of their daily lives and their own service delivery' and that this adaptation would require 'adaptation of the procedures in favour of Aboriginal processes and away from the European administrative rationalism that drives them.'[42] He adds, 'more effective delivery of welfare lies not in more efficient bureaucracy but in changing the structure of delivery to accommodate Aboriginal ways of doing things.'[43]

These cultural forms are resisting European influence.

> Aboriginal culture is changing under the influence of European post-colonialism, but it is not everywhere breaking down, or assimilating to European forms. The reaction to disintegrative pressure is the constant attempt at re-establishment of Aboriginal cultural forms.[44]

What Sullivan highlights is the need to allow self-induced adaptation of institutions into Indigenous communities. He warns against the blind imposition of the institutions of the dominant culture into Indigenous communities. He argues that the imposition of European institutions and demand for European behaviour will defeat self-determination and self-government. Patrick Sullivan has observed this process: 'It must be a slow self-generating process occurring as a result of the manipulation and resolution of ambiguities by Aborigines themselves which arise out of their interactions with Europeans.'[45] He elaborates:

> If the conditions for organic development are encouraged it will take two forms. On the one hand Aboriginal practices that were previously relatively loosely codified and open to variation will become institutionalised and applied to new forums for which there is no traditional precedent. On the other hand, these practices will be recognised, legitimated and endorsed by the dominant European political system. Only by the modernisation of Aboriginal culture can effective de-colonisation of Aborigines proceed.[46]

---

42 P Sullivan, 1996, *All Free Men Now: Culture, Community and Politics in the Kimberley Region, North-Western Australia,* Australian Institute of Aboriginal and Torres Strait Islander Studies Report Series, Australian Institute of Aboriginal and Torres Strait Islander Studies, pp 66–7.

43 Sullivan, 1996, p 67.

44 Sullivan, 1996, p 76.

45 Sullivan, 1996, p 123.

46 Sullivan, 1996, p 125.

The advantage of Sullivan's approach is that it could provide for pockets of experimental self-governance while allowing for the representation at a higher level. This would need an institutional arrangement that would allow for the delegations of powers from State and federal governments, coupled with non-discriminatory recognition and rights of citizenship.

These delegations of power are the seeds of regional agreements. They are the first step towards providing a framework for regional self-sufficiency. There has been some confusion between the talk of a treaty and the development of regional agreements, often facilitated by the use of the term 'framework agreement' to describe both processes. These delegations of power can be pursued as a solid start to the development of regional agreements for self-determination and self-government. This can take place concurrently with the negotiation of an agreed process at a national level, perhaps resulting in a treaty that provides principles and jurisdiction that will guide regional and local processes. Regional and local negotiations should be concluded on the understanding that they will be held to the standards set by the national or treaty process so that regional and local self-determination and self-government models will not fall *below* those standards.

The advantage of this coordinated, two-front national and regional approach is that regional autonomy is not put on hold until a national treaty process is resolved. It will also allow for the application of national principles to ensure these important features:

- an equality of results;
- the establishment of fundamental principles and minimum standards that regional agreements cannot fall below;
- a united and therefore more powerful political front from which Indigenous people can negotiate.

In Australia, Indigenous people have no treaty-derived powers, no recognition of their inherent right to self-government, no constitutional powers or jurisdiction in which to deal with their own affairs. For this reason, Indigenous people need a land base on which they can run community-based programs and to facilitate this institutional experimentalism. Regional agreements between government and communities that grant powers similar to that of local councils could also be a model that would allow power to be concentrated in a local community by providing Indigenous communities a base from which to negotiate with government and industry over a wide range of issues, including land title and management, resource exploitation, environmental control and the delivery of services. The untapped potential of regional agreements to secure economic development and increased rights protection has been noted by Peter Yu, former CEO of the Kimberley Land Council:

> Regional empowerment is the loom for successful weaving of indigenous rights into the national economic and social fabric, repairing the threadbare rips of chronic disadvantage. It is the key ingredient to a reconciled Australia. When I raise the concept of regional governance I am not advocating some form of separatism, but quite the opposite. It is a mechanism that will empower Aboriginal people to negotiate our inclusion and participation in the society and economies we share with our non-Aboriginal neighbours ... In my view the important feature of Indigenous governance is that it combines traditional authority with western notions of political power. Through this indigenous people can maintain the distinctive and unique dimensions of our culture and society as well as negotiate equitable relationships ...[47]

♦ ♦ ♦

As I noted earlier in this chapter, these are just some examples of how trajectories develop with a structured vision of moving from smaller, short-term goals to longer-term goals. They also highlight a rights matrix. That is, that after more than 200 years of colonisation, there can be no one solution to all the issues and that there needs to be a concerted, multifaceted approach to Indigenous rights protection. Related to this is the interplay between the rights agenda and economic development. There is a clear link between practical reconciliation and the rights framework. A rights framework without economic development will not provide the immediate responses needed at the grass-roots community level. However, targeted government policies and grass-roots initiatives that seek to improve the socio-economic position of Indigenous communities must also consider the broader legal framework into which they are created. Otherwise Indigenous communities, their programs and policies will remain vulnerable to legislative whim.

---

47 P Yu, 2001, 'Unfinished Business — National responsibilities and local actions', in S Garkawe, W Fisher and L Kelly (eds), *Indigenous Human Rights*, Federation Press, p 251.

Chapter 7
Some conclusions

> Australia's real test as far as the rest of the world, and particularly our region, is concerned, is the role we create for our own Aborigines. More than any foreign aid program, more than any international obligation which we meet or forfeit, more than any part we play in any treaty or agreement or alliance, Australia's treatment of her Aboriginal people will be the thing upon which the rest of the world will judge Australia and Australians — not just now, but in the greater perspective of history ... The Aborigines are a responsibility we cannot escape, cannot share, cannot shuffle off; the world will not let us forget that.
>
> Hon EG Whitlam, AC QC (Prime Minister 1972-75)

The Opening Ceremony to the 2000 Olympic Games in Sydney showed a distinctive style of Australian nationalism, one that acknowledged the Indigenous presence in Australia — on terms set by Indigenous people. Indigenous dancing and music in the ceremony was determined by members of the Indigenous people's own community and so truly reflected an Indigenous expression of their culture. Indigenous sprinter Cathy Freeman provided one of the finest moments of the Sydney Olympic games when she lit the Olympic flame during that ceremony.

Many foreign journalists sought to investigate the stark realities for Indigenous Australians that hid behind the projected images of the Olympic Games, but few realised how contentious and contested those symbols of unity during the opening ceremony actually were. It is this tension, this unsettled relationship, this 'unfinished business' that Australia is left to navigate now that the gaze of the international media has turned elsewhere.

As Cathy Freeman's practice of carrying of two flags (Australian and Aboriginal) symbolises, Indigenous people are seeking inclusion and recognition of difference in their relationship with Australia. Indigenous people sought symbolic inclusion in Australia's Constitution in 1967. At that time, members of Indigenous community believed that formal equality would allow Aboriginal and Torres Strait Islander people access to society and a chance to improve their socio-economic position. Over 30 years later, Indigenous leaders, activists and jurists are confronted with statistics that continually put Indigenous people at the lowest rung of the societal ladder and with a legal system that works to deprive Indigenous peoples of their rights rather than enforce them. Though it might seem, on the face of it, that Australian laws treat Indigenous people the same as other Australians, this has been far from the historical reality. In the words of poet and activist Kevin Gilbert:

> We've never been a part of the white Australian mainstream of life. Every time we've tried to join it, we've been shunted off. The only way we could join it is by becoming imitation white men. And I think that if a man has to almost prostitute himself in order to join something, he's better off without joining and by maintaining his own separate identity. The people should be in a position to make and implement their own laws and live by them, rather than have other laws forced on them.[1]

Australia's property laws, criminal justice system, Constitution and education system are entrenched with ideologies and bias. This ideology is evidenced in Australia's self-image, the nationalist identity. Not long unhooked from its British roots, Australia has idealised image of the white man conquering Australia's landscape. This colonial myth, with its tales of discovery and exploration, of founding and battling, falsely paints an image of Australia as an empty land.

So pervasive are these ideologies that even with the overturning of the legal doctrine in the *Mabo* case, the myth of *terra nullius* flourishes. Australia is a country that became wealthy through its pastoral and mining industries. Both of these industries need land. Indigenous claims to native title of land and greater community autonomy are (erroneously) perceived as a threat to the existence of those powerful industries which believe that the granting of land to the Indigenous community locks it away from them.

This nationalist identity perpetuates the legal fiction of *terra nullius* with a psychological *terra nullius* that secured Australian soil for the British. It feeds into the notions of (white) British superiority

---

1   Gilbert, 1973, p 188.

SOME CONCLUSIONS

and justifies the theft of land and labour, leaving Indigenous people and their rights either as an historical footnote or absent completely. Nationalist sentiment provides a backdrop against which Australians view Indigenous property rights. By failing to recognise Indigenous ownership and presence, Indigenous property rights are relegated to the status of a hand-out. Native title is not seen as a property right descended from prior occupation but a welfare measure: Indigenous people, when a legitimate property right is recognised, are seen as getting something for nothing.

Due to these perceptions, Indigenous rights are vulnerable, treated differently and given less protection than their non-Indigenous equivalents. The inability to lift the legacy of colonialism from the lives of Indigenous peoples is evidence of the impotence of attempts at symbolic recognition, formal equality and piecemeal attempts to win legislative and litigation victories.

Ideology also influences the way that the criminal justice system treats Indigenous peoples. By targeting them for crimes, by giving Indigenous defendants heavier sentences and by employing practices of over-policing in Indigenous communities, the Australian criminal justice system focuses oppressively on Indigenous people. It watches them, restricts them and confines them. This also has its roots in Australia's nationalist identity. Indigenous people are seen as the enemy, as the threat to the state, the other. As such, they are viewed with suspicion and distrust. These practices which single out Indigenous peoples for oppressive, racially-based punishment combine to develop a neo-colonial state. As Chris Cunneen observes:

> The nation-state attempts to formally incorporate Indigenous peoples as citizens of the nation while at the same time presenting the claims of Indigenous peoples as a threat to the political and moral unity of the nation. The claim for sovereignty is a claim against the integrity of the state and its laws. At least one effective way of denying that claim is though a process which establishes Indigenous peoples as a law and order problem and therefore the legitimate subjects of surveillance, intervention and terrorisation.[2]

The experiences of Indigenous people since European colonisation demonstrate that seemingly neutral laws – 'one law for everyone' –

---

2 C Cunneen, 1996, 'Detention, Torture and Terror and the Australian State', in G Bird, G Martin and J Nielson (eds), *Majah: Indigenous Peoples and the Law*, Federation Press, p 37.

can instead treat people differently, and that Australian institutions, like courts, are not in fact neutral but imbued with ideology.

To counter those ideological and institutional legacies, reform to improve Indigenous rights needs to look beyond small, one-off legal victories in court cases. Without targeting the ideologies inherent in the institutions of Australian society, no attempts at reform or reconciliation will be truly effective. The improvement of quality of life for Indigenous peoples means ensuring adequate protection of their basic and fundamental rights. To achieve this, it is necessary to move beyond the model of formal equality and instead adopt a strategy of institutional change rather than one of small (unsecured) wins within the existing institutional setting.

Liberal democratic societies are based on the principle that there is broad consensus on and within the governmental structure. Where consensus is lacking, democracy is replaced by the rule of majority and the minority is marginalised. The vulnerability of Indigenous peoples and their rights to popularist and legislative whim means that the focus for Indigenous peoples should be on strategies for power-sharing and nation-building. These avenues give Indigenous people stronger elements of self-determination though various models that allow decision-making by Indigenous peoples at grass-roots levels. Internal self-determination in these forms empowers state actors as they have their legitimacy increased by the incorporation of Indigenous citizens through these consensus-building and nation building projects.

In choosing which direction forward it should take as a nation, Australia has been locked in a debate between two forms of liberalism: a difference-blind liberalism and multicultural liberalism. These two liberalisms correspond to the competing images of Australia identity, the monocultural, white Australia and the new multicultural Australia. These two types of liberalism are seen as conflicting: the first, a monocultural difference-blind liberalism, will not admit allowances of difference for they may be unfair; the second, a multicultural liberalism, believes that the recognition of difference is the only way to counter the problems of formal equality. The ongoing debate between these two competing liberalisms, these two competing views of Australia, has closed off a larger set of institutional possibilities.

There is, however, another option that we can consider as a more effective way forward: an outcome-focused hybrid of the two competing paradigms which embraces both the principle of equality promoted by difference-blind liberalism and the accommodation of difference through participation of multicultural liberalism.

SOME CONCLUSIONS

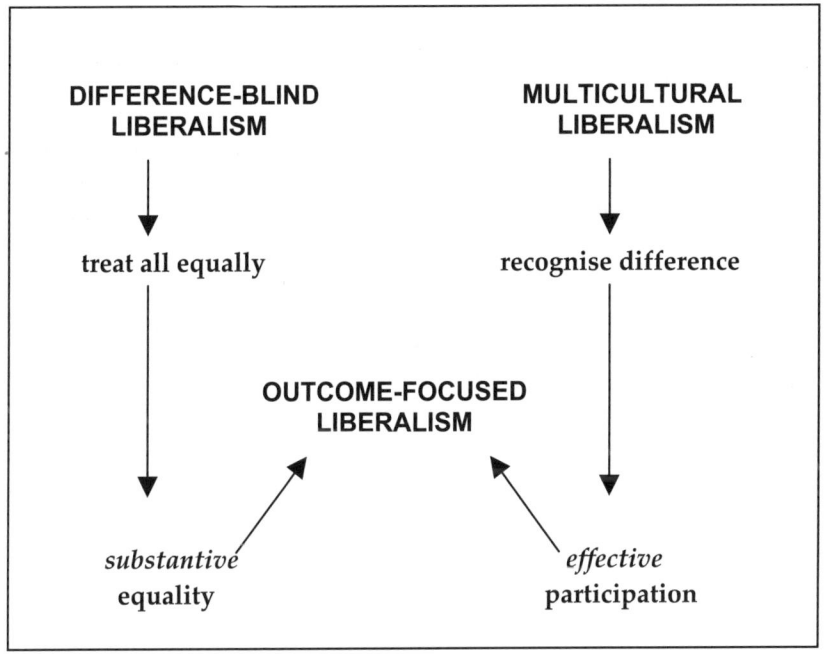

This outcome-focused liberalism rescues the notion of equality from the formal equality of difference-blind liberalism but reinterprets it as a *substantive* equality. This substantive equality is a way of acknowledging (and countering) the ideological content of the institutional arrangements within society.

Outcome-focused liberalism also rescues the notion of participation from the difference-based liberalism. This *effective* participation will allow an institutional form to be given to the recognition of difference that most multicultural communities do not allow. This will counter the greatest problem with multiculturalism: that it fails to give substantive institutional form to differences. This outcome-focused liberalism will facilitate institutional change guided by the principles of substantive equality and effective participation. It therefore seeks to alter the institutions imbued with a psychological *terra nullius* which perpetuates inequalities and historical legacies.

◆ ◆ ◆

Any attempt at reform which will improve the situation of Indigenous people must be done with consultation processes that can define what Indigenous communities need. Without this, the end results of such reform may totally fail to meet the expectations of the Indigenous communities and be ineffective in alleviating alienation and suffering. This has been the experience with almost every past government policy that did not seek to include Indigenous people in their formulation. Many of these paternalistic practices have resulted in laws and legislation that breached the rights and interests of Indigenous people, their families and their communities.

Articulating the needs of the Indigenous community is an important starting point. It is important to understand the parameters of the Indigenous claims and ask: What is it that Indigenous people are seeking?

In Indigenous political rhetoric about future aspirations, the terms sovereignty and self-determination continue to be employed to describe a range of aspirations and outcomes. This means that there needs to be a dialogue that unravels the claims within those concepts. This is a crucial step because it not only allows a starting point for reform and experimentalism, but it can also reveal that the political claims and aspirations held by the Indigenous people are not as fracturing, antagonistic or impractical as sectors of the Australian community have asserted.

In deciphering these notions of sovereignty and self determination, it becomes evident that these terms when employed in Indigenous political discussions have developed a specific definition to Aboriginal and Torres Strait Islander people. Sovereignty and self-determination are terms used to describe aspirations as broad ranging as the recognition of past injustices, greater community autonomy, protection of property interests in the land and sea, compensation for dispossession, the protection of cultural practices and recognition of customary laws and the equal protection of rights.

The notion of Indigenous sovereignty and the exercise of self-determination aim at increased autonomy, self-government and self-sufficiency *within* their communities and *within* broader Australian society. This is an agenda that seeks ways to allow for equality but also for recognition of difference and it vests decision-making power at those community levels. Indigenous people, at least on Australia's mainland, generally do not have aspirations of secession and do not seek separation from the Australian state.

SOME CONCLUSIONS

The principles of substantive equality and effective participation should guide the Indigenous agenda that seeks to achieve these aspirations. The pursuit of these democratic principles will not only ensure a framework that will target the aspirations of Indigenous communities but it will also allow for the development of a broader, more inclusive program of institutional reform, a process that will benefit other minority groups in society. This allows the Indigenous agenda to gain much needed public support.

Even with a broader, more inclusive project of institutional change, Indigenous people remain central as energetic and effective agents of transformative structural change. With the least to lose from transformation of societal institutions and their attached ideologies, they are the least likely within the community to idolise existing institutional forms. Their lack of loyalty to usually unquestioned societal structures means that an enthusiastic exploration of institutional alternatives is more likely from Indigenous groups (and other minorities) than from groups who benefit from the *status quo*.

In order to develop an effective Indigenous rights agenda, a strategic program of institutional change needs to be developed.

The first steps towards visionary aims and aspirations are sometimes only small, almost trivial, changes within Australia's legal system. This model of institutional change embraces the idea that the most effective way of achieving transformative results is to map short-term, more achievable goals and strategically link them to long-term, aspirational changes.

In relation to the Indigenous rights agenda, these short-term steps could include:

- the symbolic recognition of past injustices and Indigenous presence;
- a treaty-making process to facilitate a re-negotiation of the relationship between Indigenous people and the rest of Australia;
- an improved education system that provides an understanding of Indigenous history, wisdom and perspectives to all Australians as well as providing increased access to Indigenous people;
- improvement of affirmative action programs so that they more accurately target the disadvantaged within identified sectors of the community;
- a strengthening of the protection of Indigenous property rights, including a broad interpretation of property (in keeping with Australian law), the protection from extinguishment without

compensation, and the application of the *Racial Discrimination Act 1975* (Cth) to all dealings with native title;
- the protection of cultural practice and the recognition of customary law;
- a delegation of power towards the grass-roots community level;
- increased alliance building that creates political alliances with other sectors of the community who would also benefit from transformative institutional changes;
- a legislative Bill of Rights;
- increased rights protection under international law through compliance with the requirements of the UN committee system, the incorporation of international norms into Australian domestic law through the referencing in legislation and the continued presence and advocacy of Indigenous people in the international arena.

These steps can all strategically work towards longer-term goals, including:
- a preamble to the Constitution that recognises Indigenous presence, sovereignty, prior ownership and historical treatment;
- a national framework agreement or treaty between Indigenous people and all other Australians that should be negotiated at the national level;
- reshaping the national self-image to create a more inclusive vision of what it means to be Australian;
- economic redistribution that seeks to place more resources in the control of the economically disadvantaged;
- the development of and experimentation with alternative institutional forms;
- the negotiation of Regional Framework Agreements that assist with self-government at a local level;
- a more energised politics that facilitates increased participation in the political process by broad but often marginalised sectors of the community;
- greater protection of human rights, including constitutional protection.

It is important to remember that these areas of reform are interrelated, working together with these three identified areas:

SOME CONCLUSIONS

- *short term policies* to improve access to services and alienate socio-economic disparity;
- *economic development* to ensure long-term sustainability;
- a strengthened legal framework.

To counter the impacts and legacies of colonisation, there needs to be a holistic approach to the protection of Indigenous rights. This means that the either/or tension that has developed between practical reconciliation and the rights framework needs to be rejected and replaced by strategies, initiatives and policies that seek to develop a better understanding about the relationship between economics and rights. Just as Indigenous political responses have focused both on inclusion and special recognition, viewed as complementary rather than antagonistic elements, the approach to the tension between rights and economic development needs to be undertaken in the same holistic manner.

Practical reconciliation fails to understand the institutional barriers to substantive equality and also fails to understand that policy changes on how money will be spent cannot effect structural changes that will allow communities to break from a welfare dependency.

At the same time, advocates of the rights framework need to focus more intently on the economic rights that can and should be promoted within such a framework. Better links need to be formed between the rhetoric, substance and form of rights protection and the placing of food on the table, better health, clean water, suitable housing and access to educational and employment opportunities.

Lessons must also be learned from the Canadian experience where rights protection has been improved through the introduction of specific legal mechanisms. Advocates of the rights framework must also concentrate on ensuring that recognition of rights that appear on paper are filtered into Indigenous communities in a tangible way. Ensuring that such transmission occurs will ease emerging scepticism about the rights framework as a workable, practical and useful solution.

Until the relevance of the rights framework becomes clear to those who need its protection the most, the changes that go to the heart of overturning the psychological *terra nullius* still pervasive in Australia's Constitution, laws and policies will not gain the support required to implement them.

♦ ♦ ♦

Indigenous people have broken through the social and legal barricades that barred them from equal citizenship rights but formal equality has been a disappointing framework for achieving equality and expression of the way in which Indigenous people want to live their lives authentically. Formal equality has not offered full realisation of Indigenous aspirations for greater community autonomy or true equal rights and status.

This failure of the model of formal equality raises a question that all Australians need to consider: If the laws and institutions of Australia do not work for the most disadvantaged and marginalised sector of the community, the Indigenous people, are they good enough? The continual relegation of Indigenous Australians to the lowest rung of the socio-economic ladder not only demands that all Australians come to terms with their history and their ideals, it requires a critical questioning of what democracy means in Australia. Australians need to assess, against the experiences and treatment of Indigenous Australians, what it means to be Australian, the vision of the kind of country they wish to live in and the principles that Australia needs to govern by.

The role played by Indigenous people in assessing the performance and effectiveness of Australian democracy is a role that Felix Cohen suggested for Native Americans in the United States.

> The Indian plays the same role in our American society that the Jews played in Germany. Like the miner's canary, the Indian marks the shift from fresh air to poison gas in our political atmosphere; and our treatment of Indians, even more than our treatment of other minorities reflects the rise and fall of democratic faith.[3]

Indigenous people are Australia's 'miner's canary'. The practical outcome of using Indigenous experiences as a measurement of the effectiveness of how well Australian society is working is one that will require an investigation and understanding of those unique Indigenous experiences, histories and identities. This renewed focus will help to undermine the psychological *terra nullius* that has worked to make Indigenous people virtually invisible from the dominant colonial images of Australian nationalism entrenched in its institutions.

Australians need to look to the Indigenous community not merely for the richness of Indigenous culture nor to appropriate

---

3 F Cohen, 1960, 'Anthropology and the Problems of Indian Administration', in L Cohen (ed), *The Legal Conscience: Selected Papers of Felix S Cohen*, Yale University Press, p 202.

SOME CONCLUSIONS

symbols to impress the world with its cultural diversity but to find ways to enrich Australia's institutional framework. Pathways towards improved Indigenous rights protections will provide results that will transform Australia's legal and political institutions in ways that will offer improved rights protections, opportunities and inclusion to the whole community. To this end, the Indigenous political agenda will lead to the creation of institutions that benefit *all* members of Australian society.

Bibliography

Aboriginal and Torres Strait Islander Social Justice Commission (ATSISJC), 1993, *First Report 1993*, Australian Government Publishing Service.

Aboriginal and Torres Strait Islander Commission (ATSIC), 1995, *Annual Report 1994-1995*, Australian Government Publishing Service.

Aboriginal and Torres Strait Islander Commission (ATSIC), 1999, *Indigenous Australians Today*, Aboriginal and Torres Strait Islander Commission.

Anaya, S James, 1996, *Indigenous Peoples in International Law*, Oxford University Press.

Appleby, J, Hunt L and Jacob, M, 1994, *Telling the Truth About History*, WW Norton.

Attwood, B, and Markus A (eds), 1999, *The Struggle for Aboriginal Rights: A Documentary History*, Allen & Unwin.

Australian Bureau of Statistics, 1997a, *1996 Census of Population and Housing*, Australian Government Publishing Service.

Australian Bureau of Statistics, 1997b, *Cultural Trends in Australia*, Australian Government Publishing Service.

Australian Bureau of Statistics, *Australia Now – A Statistical Profile of Australia 2000* (www.abs.gov.au)

Australian Law Reform Commission, 1986, *Report into the Recognition of Aboriginal Customary Law*, Australian Government Publishing Service.

Baldwin, J, 1963, *The Fire Next Time*, Dial Press.

Behrendt, J and Behrendt L, 'Aboriginal Deaths in Custody Since the Royal Commission', 2(59) (December 1992a) *Aboriginal Law Bulletin* 4.

Behrendt, J and Behrendt L, 1992b, 'Aborigines and the Police: Bad Apples or Rotten Fruit?', 14 April *Tharunka* 14.

Behrendt, L, 1995, *Aboriginal Dispute Resolution*, Federation Press.

Behrendt, P, 1995, 'Aboriginal Sovereignty: Australian Republic: A Catalogue of Questions and Answers', in I Moores (ed), *The Voices of Aboriginal Australia: Past, Present, Future*, Butterfly Books.

Berger, J, 1988, *Aborigines Today: Land and Justice*, Anti-Slavery Society.

Burney, L, 2000, 'Not Just a Challenge, an Opportunity', in M Grattan (ed), *Reconciliation*, Black Ink.

Clark, G, 2000a, 'Native Title and the Political Environment', in L Strelein and K Muir (eds), *Native Title in Perspective: Selected Papers from the Native Title Research Unit 1998–2000*, Native Title Research Unit, Australian Institute of Aboriginal and Torres Strait Islander Studies.

Clark, G, 2000b, 'Not Much Progress', in M Grattan (ed), *Reconciliation*, Black Ink.

Cohen, F, 1960, 'Anthropology and the Problems of Indian Administration', in L Cohen (ed), *The Legal Conscience: Selected Papers of Felix S Cohen*, Yale University Press.

Cope, B, 1987, *Racism, Popular Culture and Australian Identity in Transition: a Case Study of Change in School Textbooks Since 1945*, Common Ground.

Cunneen, C, 1996, 'Detention, Torture and Terror and the Australian State', in G Bird, G Martin and J Nielson (eds), *Majah: Indigenous Peoples and the Law*, Federation Press.

Cunneen, C, and T Libesman, 1995, *Indigenous People and the Law in Australia*, Butterworths.

Davies, A, 1997, 'Bluebloods fund Libs with blue-chip shares', *Sydney Morning Herald*, 23 December.

Davies, AF, 1988, *Three Essays in Political Psychology*, McPhee Gribble, Penguin Books.

Dewey, J, 1927, *The Public and Its Problems*, Ohio University Press

Dodson, M, 1995, Aboriginal and Torres Strait Islander Social Justice Commission, *Introductory Remarks*, United Nations Procedures and Indigenous Australians, Sydney, 28 June.

Dodson, P, 1996, 'Reconciliation Misunderstood', *The Australian*, 13 September, p 12.

Dodson, P, 2000, 'Until the Chains are Broken', 4th Vincent Lingiari Memorial Lecture, in M Grattan (ed), *Essays on Reconciliation*, Black Inc.

Dodson, P, 2000, 'Beyond the Mourning Gate — Dealing with Unfinished Business', 12th Wentworth Lecture, Australian Institute of Aboriginal and Torres Strait Islander Studies.

Douglas, M, 1986, *How Institutions Think*, Syracuse University Press.

Federal Race Discrimination Commissioner, 1997, *Face the Facts*, Federal Race Discrimination Commissioner.

Gilbert, K, 1973, *Because a White Man Will Never Do It*, Angus & Robertson.

Gilbert K, 1987, draft treaty, reproduced in Attwood and Markus, 1999, pp 312-13.

Goodall, H, 1996, *Invasion to Embassy: Land in Aboriginal Politics in New South Wales, 1770–1972*, Allen & Unwin.

'Governor calls for 'recognition', *Sydney Morning Herald*, 3 June 1997, p 5.

'Governor joins call for apology', *Sydney Morning Herald*, 3 June 1997.

Grattan, M (ed), 2000, *Reconciliation*, Black Ink.

Harris, T, 1996, 'One in three jailed juveniles Aboriginal', *The Weekend Australian*, 26–27 October, p8.

Havnen, O, 2000, 'The Native Title Amendment Act', in L Strelein and K Muir (eds), *Native Title in Perspective: Selected Papers from the Native Title Research Unit 1998–2000*, Native Title Research Unit, Australian Institute of Aboriginal and Torres Strait Islander Studies.

'History, white or wrong?', *Sydney Morning Herald*, 26 October 1996, p 33.

Howard, J, 2000a, "Address to Participants at the Longreach Community Meeting to Discuss the Wik 10 Point Plan, Longreach, Queensland",

BIBLIOGRAPHY

reproduced in Parliamentary Joint Committee on Native Title and the Aboriginal and Torres Strait Islander Land Fund, 2000, *CERD and the Native Title Amendment Act 1998*, Parliament of the Commonwealth of Australia.

Howard, J, 2000b, Address at the presentation of the Final Report to Federal Parliament by the Council for Aboriginal Reconciliation, 7 December.

Howard, J, 2000c, *Menzies Lecture Series: Perspectives on Aboriginal and Torres Strait Islander Issues*, 13 December.

Human Rights and Equal Opportunity Commission (HREOC), 1997, *Bringing Them Home: A Guide to the Findings and Recommendations of the National Inquiry into the Separation of Aboriginal and Torres Strait Islander Children from their Families*, Australian Government Publishing Service.

Human Rights and Equal Opportunity Commission (HREOC), 1999, *Social Justice Report 1999*, Human Rights and Equal Opportunity Commission.

Interviews with author
L Bellear, 27 August 1997
T Birch, 23 January 2003
K-R Gilbert, 22 January 2003
M McMillan, 18 January 2003
G Scott, 7 January 2003
R Sykes, 20 December 1997

'Jail shake-up keeps blacks out of cells', *Sydney Morning Herald*, 19 November 1996.

'Jawoyn launch five-year plan', *ATSIC News*, April 1997.

Jopson, D, 2000, 'Vote of confidence, now Clark battles on', *Sydney Morning Herald*, 16 August, p 4.

Jopson, D, and I Verrender, 1997, 'Richest of Rich are Wik Winners', *Sydney Morning Herald*, 10 May.

Kalantzis, M, 2000, Paper delivered at *Unchain My Mind: New Social-Democratic Ideas for Labor in Government*, 27 July, Trades Hall, Melbourne.

Langton, M, 1994, 'Indigenous Self-Government and Self-Determination: Overlapping Jurisdiction at Cape York', in C Fletcher (ed), *Aboriginal Self-Determination in Australia*, Australian Institute of Aboriginal and Torres Strait Islander Studies.

'Law Must Dig Deeper to Find Land Rights', *The Australian*, 8 June 1993.

Letter to the Editor, *Sydney Morning Herald*, 18 August 2000, p 15.

'Literary crisis for outback Aborigines', *Sydney Morning Herald*, 19 October 1996, p 13.

Lui, G, 1994, 'Self-Government in the Torres Strait Islands', in C Fletcher (ed), *Aboriginal Self-Determination in Australia*, Australian Institute of Aboriginal and Torres Strait Islander Studies.

Mackay, H, 1988, *Mackay Report: Being Australian: March 1988*, Mackay Research Centre for Communication Studies.

Mackay, H, 1999, *Turning Point: Australian's Choosing Their Future*, Macmillan.

Madden, R, 1995, *National Aboriginal and Torres Strait Islander Survey, 1994*, Australian Bureau of Statistics.

Manning, I, 1997, *Native Title, Mining, and Mineral Exploration*, National Institute of Economic Industry and Research.

Mansell, M, 1994, 'Taking Control of Resources', in C Fletcher (ed), *Aboriginal Self-Determination in Australia*, Australian Institute of Aboriginal and Torres Strait Islander Studies.

McCulloch, J, 'Mandatory Sentencing: Creating an Incarcerated Generation', 47 (June-July 2000) *Arena Magazine*, p 33.

McMinn, WG, 1994, *Nationalism and Federalism in Australia*, Oxford University Press.

McRae, H, G Nettheim and L Beacroft, 1991, *Aboriginal Legal Issues: Commentary and materials*, Law Book.

Mill, JS, 1993 (orig 1859), *On Liberty and Utilitarianism*, Bantam Books.

Minister for Foreign Affairs (Alexander Downer), press release, 30 March 2000.

Minister for Foreign Affairs (Alexander Downer), Attorney-General (The Hon Daryl Williams AM QC MP), Minister for Immigration and Multicultural Affairs (The Hon Philip Ruddock MP), Joint media release, Tuesday, 29 August 2000, FA97.

Minow, M, 1990, *Making All the Difference: inclusion, exclusion and American Law*, Cornell University Press.

Morgan, H, 1992, 'The Dangers of Aboriginal Sovereignty', *News Weekly*, 29 August, p 13.

'Mr Howard unreconciled', *Sydney Morning Herald*, 27 May 1997, p 14.

Mundine, D, 1999, 'The Land is Full of Signs: Central North East Arnham Land Art', in H Morphy and M Smith Boles (eds), *Art of the Land*, University of Virginia Press.

Munro, J, 1995, 'Aboriginal Deaths in Custody Result from the Paternalistic Status Quo', in I Moores (ed), *Voices of Aboriginal Australia: Past, Present, Future*, Butterfly Books.

National Aboriginal Island Health Organization (NAIHO), 1985, Written comment, NAIHO Conference, <www.kooriweb.org/foley/news/story8.html>, accessed 19 December 2002.

Pearce, D, 1994,'Aboriginal Self Government', in C Fletcher (ed), *Aboriginal Self-Determination in Australia*, Australian Institute of Aboriginal and Torres Strait Islander Studies.

Pearson, N, 2000, 'Aboriginal Disadvantage', in M Grattan (ed), *Reconciliation*, Black Ink.

Perkins, C, 1994, 'Self Determination and Managing the Future', in C Fletcher (ed), *Aboriginal Self-Determination in Australia*, Australian Institute of Aboriginal and Torres Strait Islander Studies.

Pike, W, 2000, Letter to the Editor, *Sydney Morning Herald*, 19 July.

'Racing towards an election', *Sydney Morning Herald*, 11 April 1998.

'PM's apology draws protest', *Sydney Morning Herald*, 27 May 1997.

Ramsey A, 1997, 'Ramsey's View: Conflict of interest? So what?', *Sydney Morning Herald*, 10 May.

BIBLIOGRAPHY

'Republicans, Bludgers and Hyenas – Ruxton Celebrates,' *Sydney Morning Herald*, 3 July 1997, p12

Reynolds, H, 1982, *The Other Side of the Frontier: Aboriginal Resistance to the European Invasion of Australia*, Penguin.

Reynolds, H, 1992, *The Law of the Land*, Penguin.

Roche, D, 1999, *Mandatory Sentencing*, Trends and Issues in Crime and Criminal Justice No 138, Australian Institute of Criminology.

Royal Commission into Aboriginal Deaths in Custody (RCIADIC), 1989, *Report of the Inquiry into the Death of Malcolm Charles Smith*, Australian Government Publishing Service.

Royal Commission into Aboriginal Deaths in Custody (RCIADIC), 1990, *Report of the Inquiry into the Death of Harrison Day*, Australian Government Publishing Service.

Royal Commission into Aboriginal Deaths in Custody (RCIADIC), 1991, *National Report: Overview and Recommendations*, Australian Government Publishing Service.

Seccombe, M, and G Roberts, 1998, 'Mining His Own Business', *Sydney Morning Herald*, 21 March.

Skehan, C, 1997, 'Amnesty targets law in Report', *Sydney Morning Herald*, 19 June.

Skelton, R, and G Roberts, 1998, 'Parer crisis escalates as Japan meeting revealed', *Sydney Morning Herald*, 20 March.

Sullivan, P, 1996, *All Free Men Now: Culture, Community and Politics in the Kimberley Region, North-Western Australia*, Australian Institute of Aboriginal and Torres Strait Islander Studies.

'The sooner we get this debate over the better for all of us', *The Age*, 1 December 1997.

The Sun News-Pictorial, 1949, *Wonderful Australia in Pictures*, Herald and Weekly Times.

Taylor, C, 1994, *Multiculturalism: examining the politics of recognition*, Princeton University Press.

Tingle, L, 1998, 'Parer linked to new mine group', *Sydney Morning Herald*, 24 March.

Unger, R, 1996, *What Should Legal Analysis Become?*, Verso.

United Nations, UN Doc. E/CN4/Sub2/1994/L60, 24 August 1994.

United Nations, UN Doc. E/CN4/Sub2/1993/29/Annex I, 23 August 1993.

United Nations Committee on the Elimination of all forms of Racial Discrimination CERD/C/54/Misc40/Rev2, March 1991.

United Nations Committee on the Elimination of all forms of Racial Discrimination CERD/C/56/Misc42/Rev3, 2000.

'Wadjularbinna Nulyarimma', interview with Caroline Jones, reproduced in I Moores (ed), 1995, *Voices of Aboriginal Australia: Past, Present, Future*, Butterfly Books. Williams, G, 1999, *Human Rights under the Australian Constitution*, Oxford University Press.

'Why we can't sleep soundly', *Sydney Morning Herald*, 28 May 1997, p 17.

Williams, G, 2000, *A Bill of Rights for Australia*, University of New South Wales Press.

Wilson, M, 2000, Letter to the Editor, *Sydney Morning Herald*, 19 July.

Woodford, J, 1996, 'Family's land dream turns into nightmare', *Sydney Morning Herald*, 24 December, p 1.

Woodford, J, 1997, 'Native Title's $1bn victory', *Sydney Morning Herald*, 28 March.

Yu, P, 2000, 'Unfinished Business — National responsibilities and local actions', address given at Southern Cross University (NSW), 12 February, in S Garkawe and L Kelly (eds), *Indigenous Human Rights*, Federation Press, p 251.

Yunupingu, G, 1987, 'What the Aboriginal People Want' *Age*, 26 August, page no?, reprinted in B Attwood and A Markus (eds), 1999, *The Struggle for Aboriginal Rights: A Documentary History*, Allen & Unwin, p 314.

Yunupingu, M, 1994, 'Give Back Our Laws', *Herald* Sun, 25 January, p 4.

Index

10 point plan, 2, 45-46, 53
1967 Referendum, 1, 7, 13, 14, 29, 31, 127, 170
Aboriginal and Torres Strait Islander people
  criminal justice system, 8, 21-28, 122
  education, 1, 7, 8, 12, 56, 71-76, 88, 91, 93, 101, 124, 125, 126, 132, 136-138, 148, 156, 175
  employment, 7, 8, 72, 88, 91, 124, 125, 156
  family violence, 124-125
  health, 7, 8, 12, 70, 88, 118, 124, 125, 126, 148, 156
  housing, 35, 124, 148
  juveniles, 23, 24
  life expectancy, 7
  mortality rate, 7
  negative stereotypes, 23, 43, 45, 65-66
  poverty, 7-8, 63, 88, 126
  women, 23, 26
Aboriginal and Torres Strait Islander Commission (ATSIC), 22, 49, 102, 105
Aboriginal Education Consultative Group (AECG), 164-164
Aboriginal Land Rights Act 1983 (NSW), 38-40
Aboriginal Provisional Government (APG), 86, 97-98, 102-103, 119
Aboriginal Tent Embassy, 14, 19
Aboriginal identity, 15, 17, 19, 55, 62, 77, 79, 83, 88, 90
Aborigines Protection Board (APB), 1, 4, 37, 67-71, 72, 136
Anaya, S James, 127-128
apology, 75, 93, 133, 150
Appleby, Joyce, 75
assimilation, 54, 71, 72
Australian Bureau of Statistics (ABS), 7-8, 58
Australian Law Reform Commission (ALRC), 26
Australian Democrat Party, 46, 142
Baldwin, James, 56
Barunga Statement, 87-89, 90, 93, 94, 114-115, 146, 149
Behrendt, Jason, 130

Behrendt, Larissa, 130
Behrendt, Paul, 33, 95, 108, 112
Bellear, Lisa, 98
Bill of Rights, 116, 124, 132, 145-149, 158
Birch, Tony, 108
Bringing them Home Report *see also* Stolen Generations, 4, 5, 59, 62, 63, 67-71
Burney, Linda, 107
Clark, Geoff, 51, 90, 93, 94, 109, 118-119, 120
Cohen, Felix, 178
communitarianism, 78-79
Constitution, 8, 13, 28, 30, 31, 52, 54, 92, 93, 104, 116, 122, 124, 132, 133, 141-145, 157-159, 170, 176, 177
  acquisitions power, s 51(xxxi), 52
  external affairs power, s 51 (xxix), 152
  non-discrimination clause (proposed), 30, 159
  preamble, 60, 116, 124, 132, 141-145, 158
  races power, s 51(xxvi), 1, 6, 29, 31, 164, 165
  section 25, 158
Cope, Bill, 74
Council for Aboriginal Reconciliation (CAR), 9-10, 27
Convention for the Elimination of all forms of Discrimination Against Women (CEDAW), 147-156
Convention for the Elimination of all forms of Racial Discrimination (CERD), 12, 13, 26, 53, 88, 106, 115, 146-147, 150, 152
Cubillo, Lorna, 10, 145
cultural protection, 91, 92, 96, 113, 116, 124, 148, 156
Cunneen, Chris, 23, 171
customary law,26, 88, 89, 91, 92, 93, 113-114, 116, 123, 124, 132, 141, 156
Davies, AF, 64
Day, Harrison, 72-73
Deane, William, 4, 71
democracy, concept of,16-18, 20, 81, 102
Dewey, John,16, 84
dispossession,1, 2, 8, 34, 35-36, 39, 40, 54, 63, 106, 133, 144
Dodson, Mick, 53, 154-155
Dodson, Patrick, 90-93, 94, 107-108, 126
Douglas, Mary,120-121

INDEX

Downer, Alexander, 151
Draft Declaration on the Rights of Indigenous Peoples, 106, 154-156
economic development, 8, 91, 93, 96, 112, 113-114, 116, 124, 177
effective participation, 84, 85, 127-129, 131, 173, 175, 176
Eva Valley Statement, 87, 89-90, 92-93
formal equality, 13, 14, 19, 21, 54-55, 149, 172, 177
Fraser Government, 37
Freeman, Cathy, 62, 70-71, 169
Gilbert, Kevin, 96-97, 112-113, 170
Goodall, Heather, 33, 34, 36
Griffith, Gavan, 29-30
Gummow, William, 29
Gunner, Peter, 10, 145
Hand, Gerry, 105
Hanson, Pauline, 61
Harradine, Brian, 48
Havenan, Olga, 49, 50-51
Hawke, Bob, 87
Hayne, Kenneth, 29
heritage protection, 6, 29, 88, 89, 116, 123, 124, 148, 156
Herron, John, 46
High Court, 2, 28, 29, 41, 42, 44, 141, 152, 158
Hindmarsh Island Bridge case (Kartinyeri v Commonwealth), 6, 29, 158
Hollinsworth, David, 75
Howard, John, 2, 3, 4, 9, 10, 11, 49-50, 61, 64, 71, 75, 142
Howard Government, 13, 29, 45, 46
Human Rights and Equal Opportunity Commission (HREOC), 4, 5, 24, 25, 26, 63, 70, 103, 104, 111, 152
Hunt, Lynne, 75
identity, 76-84, 115
individualism, 77-79
institutional change, 15, 17, 19, 20, 117, 120-123, 124, 133, 138-141, 175, 176
International Covenant on Economic Social and Cultural Rights, (ICESCR), 88, 106, 115, 146, 147, 151, 156
International Covenant on Civil and Political Rights (ICCPR), 88, 106, 115, 146-147, 151, 152, 156

International Human Rights, see also Rights, 88, 89, 97, 114-115, 124, 127-128, 132, 146-147, 149-157
Jobson, Debra, 46, 118
Jacob, Margaret, 75
Kalantzis, Mary, 59-60
Kartinyeri v Commonwealth, *see* Hindmarsh Island Bridge case
Keating Government, 44
Kernot, Cheryl, 46
Kirby, Michael, 29-30, 39
Kruger v Commonwealth, 11, 12, 28, 145, 158
land rights, 33-35, 37-41, 88, 92, 96, 112-113, 123, 124, 132, 148, 175
Langton, Marcia, 111
language, 91, 92, 156
legal pluralism, 129-131, 139-140
liberalism
   difference-blind, 81-84, 172
   multicultural, 81-84, 172
   outcome-focused, 84, 173
Libesman, Teresa, 23
Lui, Getano, 102
Mabo case, 1, 3, 6, 41-44, 45, 52, 129, 140, 143, 170
Mackay, Hugh, 56, 60, 61, 63, 64-65, 66
Madden, Richard, 22, 69
mandatory sentencing, 13, 21-28, 150
Mansell, Michael, 121, 122
McMillan, Mark, 99-100
McMinn, WG, 58
Mill, John Stuart, 77
Minow, Martha, 80
Morgan, Hugh, 43, 47-48, 67
multiculturalism, 59, 60, 74, 138-139, 172
Mundine, Djon, 33
Munro, Jenny, 109
Murray, Les, 142
National Aboriginal and Islander Health Organisation (NAIHO), 100
National Aboriginal and Islander Legal Services Secretariat (NAILLS), 69

INDEX

National Native Title Tribunal, 4, 44

nationalism, 3, 6, 32, 47, 48, 55, 56-67, 75-76, 79, 115, 124, 132, 133, 138-139, 144

native title, 2, 3, 10, 29, 31-32, 41-53, 89-90, 92, 112-113, 123, 124, 132, 145, 148, 171, 175

Native Title Act 1993 (Cth), 3, 44, 48-49, 53, 90

Native Title Amendment Act 1998 (Cth), 2, 4, 13, 45-49, 50, 53, 150

Ngaanyatjarra Aboriginal Community, 160-163

Nulyarimma, Wadjularbinna, 136

O'Shane, Pat, 130

Pearce, Darryl, 163

Pearson, Noel, 51, 118-119, 120, 162, 163

Perkins, Charles, 109, 113-114

police, 23, 27

Practical Reconciliation, 9-11, 177

Psychological *terra nullius*, 3, 20, 21, 99, 108, 117, 120, 133, 135, 173

Racial Discrimination Act 1975 (Cth), 2, 44, 52, 129, 176, 177

Ramsey, Alan, 46

Reed-Gilbert, Kerry, 98-99

Regional Agreements, 15, 92, 93, 116, 124, 133, 167, 176

regional autonomy, 159-168

republic, 60, 145

Reynolds, Henry, 16, 134

rights, 6, 9, 11, 12-13, 28, 88-89, 115-116, 120, 123, 125, 126, 132-133, 144, 146-149, 176
  due process before the law, 28
  equality before the law, 28, 147
  freedom from discrimination, 89
  freedom of religion, 28
  freedom of movement, 28
  right to life, 88, 147
  right to liberty, 88, 147
  right to security of person, 88

Roche, Declan, 25

Royal Commission into Aboriginal Deaths in Custody (RCIADIC), 5, 20-24, 27, 35, 63, 69-70, 72-73, 110

Rubuntja, Wenten, 87

Ruddock, Philip, 151
Ruxton, Bruce, 59
Scott, Geoff, 105
self-determination, 18, 20, 34, 85, 86, 87-117, 121, 123, 127-128, 146, 152, 159, 167, 174
self-government, 102, 103, 144, 148, 163, 167, 174
Smith, Malcolm Charles, 69
Sovereign Aboriginal Coalition, 96, 112-113
sovereignty, 18, 20, 43, 79, 87-117, 121, 123, 133, 134, 140, 141, 144, 152, 159, 167, 171, 174
special measures, 91, 124
Stolen Generations, 1, 4, 5, 10, 11, 12, 13, 28, 29, 37, 54, 56, 63-64, 67-71, 93, 94, 106, 145
substantive equality, 13-14, 83-84, 85, 125-127, 131, 149, 173, 175
Sullivan, Patrick, 165-166
Sykes, Roberta, 101, 121
Taylor, Charles, 77-81
treaty, 15, 92, 93, 95, 104, 112-113, 116, 124, 132, 167, 175
Unger, Roberto Mangabiera, 17, 18
Universal Declaration of Human Rights, 88, 115, 146, 156
Ward, Russel, 74
welfare reform, 124, 156
Western Australian Chamber of Mines, 38
White Australia Policy, 31, 58-59, 60, 138-139, 143
Whitlam, Gough, 15, 169
Whitlam Government, 37
Wik case, 2, 3, 6, 31, 44-45, 47
Williams, Daryl, 151
Williams, George, 6, 29, 30, 142, 143
Wooldridge, Michael, 118
Wootten, Hal, 72-73
xenophobia, 60-61
Yu, Peter, 168
Yunupingu, Galarrwuy, 34-35, 87, 90, 93-94, 95
Yunupingu, Mandawuy, 113

Also available from The Federation Press:

Aboriginal Dispute Resolution

Larissa Behrendt

Behrendt argues for radical change in the way land disputes involving Aboriginal Australians are settled and proposes a new system which promotes genuine and lasting reconciliation between Aboriginal and non-Aboriginal Australians.

Writing from an Aboriginal perspective, she points out the entrenched distrust Aboriginals have of white justice, and the power imbalances present in most disputes. Giving worked examples, she proposes that land disputes involving Aboriginals should be resolved by elders on Aboriginal land using traditional Aboriginal methods.

> *Behrendt's book has little rancour but with uncompromising determination, clarity and passion, she describes the disadvantaged status of Aborigines and Torres Strait Islanders from the legal myth of* terra nullius *to the dramatic* Mabo *decision ... This book is a knowledgeable statement of facts as she sees them, simplified to facilitate understanding of a very complex and emotive issue.*
>
> Civil Liberty

> *Her account is accessible and very much a personal one – shaped essentially by here identity as an Aboriginal woman and by her previous research work. This viewpoint is critical to the strength of her work ...*
>
> Canberra Bulletin of Public Administration

> Aboriginal Dispute Resolution *is essential reading for all those who wish to work for a society that has principles of equity and natural justice as its fundamentals.*
>
> Aboriginal Law Bulletin

> *Behrendt provides the most useful insights into the manner in which non-Aboriginal parties should approach dispute resolution with Aboriginal parties, particularly in relation to land access.*
>
> Melbourne University Law Review

1995 • 1 86287 178 7 • 120pp • $19.95

Mabo, Wik & Native Title 4th edn

Peter Butt, Robert Eagleson & Patricia Lane

This book provides an accurate, accessible and unbiased account of what the judges and the Acts of Parliament have actually said about native title, what it means and what problems are likely to arise in the near future.

The book starts with a plain language version of the High Court's 1993 ruling in *Mabo,* still the basic legal document on native title, and follows with equally straightforward explanations of the *Native Title Act* 1993, the 1996 High Court judgment in *Wik*, and the Howard government's legislative response in 1998 with the "10 point plan".

Praise for earlier editions

Makes a brilliant contribution ... must find its way into the homes and schools of all Australians so that all may understand the reasoning of the High Court and the clear legal and historical basis for the decision.
Noel Pearson

... an insight into the heart of one of the most significant changes in the nation's history
Paul Keating

This text is so easy to read and to understand that I'm glad I took the trouble. I now believe I know what the judgment really said ...
Journal, Australian Institute of Professional Communicators

Reviews of the first edition were extremely complimentary but I have no hesitation in saying that this update is even better.
Law Society of Tasmania Lawletter

This book should be included as reading for everyone from high school students to politicians.
Alternative Law Journal

2001 • 1 86287 386 0 • paperback • 134pp • $24.75

The Black Grapevine
Aboriginal Activism and the Stolen Generation
Linda Briskman

The Black Grapevine tells the extraordinary story of Indigenous efforts to stop children becoming part of the 'stolen generation' and to end the government policies and practices which destroyed their families.

Linda Briskman uses the story of SNAICC to centre her book. Indigenous people involved tell how they came together to form a national organisation for child care, how they found similar experiences from one end of Australia to the other, how they pooled experience and emotion to provide support for one another, how they lobbied for a national inquiry.

And how they campaigned. Indigenous activists fought with astonishing resilience for recognition of past and present practices, for the right to have Indigenous viewpoints to the forefront, and for resources.

Briskman's story goes beyond the contest with the state to give a convincing portrait of the ways in which Indigenous groups work. There are connections with international action, educational projects, and the much-vaunted annual Aboriginal and Islander Children's Day.

She concludes by reflecting on the successes of campaigns and actions to date, and the extent of 'unfinished business' – the ongoing removal of Indigenous children from their families and the trauma still faced by those who are part of the stolen generations. Briskman's strong academic background combines with the oral testimony of the activists to produce a fast-moving book that is both entertaining and rigorous.

2003 • ISBN 1 86287 449 2 • Paperback • 224 pages • $22.95

What Are Human Rights?
Thomas Fleiner

This is extraordinarily clear and simple account of what human rights are and why they are so important ... Each of the 35 chapters begins with a little story having human rights implications, and around that story Fleiner weaves his arguments. ... In an age when human rights are on the top of the global agenda, this excellent book written in simple prose appears as a 'Bible' of human rights.
West Bengal Political Science Review

This fascinating little book ... an easy-to read-style using simple language and many stories ... Almost anywhere one dips into the book one finds reference to topical issues ... most useful and stimulating
Panorama

A clearly-written book that engages the reader through practical examples and thought-provoking anecdotes
Journal of Family Studies

Fleiner successfully presents a realistic appraisal of human rights, one that acknowledges and highlights rather than avoids the difficulties inherent in the protection of human rights.
Australian International Law Journal

Thomas Fleiner is a leading Swiss constitutional lawyer who has practical understanding of government in countries as diverse as South Africa, the USA, Russia, China & Columbia. He was for over a decade a member of the International Committee of the Red Cross and has been involved in attempts to resolve some of the most terrible modern human rights problems, most notably in the former Yugoslavia. His book has previously been published in German, Russian, French and Spanish.

1999 • ISBN • 1 86287 328 3 • Paperback • 176pp • $25.00